Winning by Losing

WINNING BY LOSING

by
RICHARD A. FOWLER

MOODY PRESS
CHICAGO

ACKNOWLEDGEMENT

I wish to thank my wife, Jerilyn, for the many hours she labored while editing this book.

© 1986 by
THE MOODY BIBLE INSTITUTE
OF CHICAGO

All Scripture quotations, unless noted otherwise, are from the *New American Standard Bible,* © 1960, 1962, 1963, 1968, 1971, 1973, 1975, and 1977 by the Lockman Foundation, and are used by permission.

Library of Congress Cataloging-in-Publication Data

Fowler, Richard A., 1948-
    Winning by losing.

    1. Christian life—1960-   I. Title.
BV4501.2.F66   1986   248.4   86-5164
ISBN 0-8024-9564-8 (pbk.)

1 2 3 4 5 6 7 Printing/BC/Year 90 89 88 87 86

Printed in the United States of America

To my godly parents,
who led me to Christ and then taught me
by their life and words what it means to walk
the Christian path. I am eternally grateful
for their persistence with me in my developmental years,
for their prayers on my behalf, and for their love.

CONTENTS

PART 5:
A MATTER OF LIFE AND DEATH

Foreword

Tevye, the old Russian Jew in *Fiddler on the Roof*, had a great capacity for seeing both sides of an issue. He had lots of practice because all his lovely daughters wanted to marry men of whom he disapproved. But his love for the girls made him reconsider. "On the one hand," he would say, "but on the other hand." When his youngest daughter arrived with her young man, however, it was too much. He looked at both sides of the argument and concluded with great anguish, "But there is no other hand!"

Christians need to look at truth the same way. Many issues do not yield simple answers. Many Scriptures do not present simple interpretation. There is a real "on the one hand, on the other hand" factor, which sometimes leads to a definite "but there is no other hand" solution.

Dr. Fowler's book addresses this issue with regard to the paradoxes of Scripture. He presents different views of difficult biblical passages and helps us come to some conclusions. Sometimes he presents a "but there is no other hand" case; sometimes he leaves us with an "on the one hand, but on the other" option. Either way, his book is helpful for those who wish to think about their faith—and for those who may never have dared to do so!

D. STUART BRISCOE

Preface

Jesus, in a prayer offered to His Father in heaven, said,

> I praise Thee, O Father, Lord of heaven and earth, that Thou didst hide these things from the wise and intelligent and didst reveal them to babes. (Matthew 11:25)

And later, while answering His disciples' question concerning the reason He spoke in parables, Jesus quoted Isaiah:

> You will keep on hearing, but will not understand; and you will keep on seeing, but will not perceive; for the heart of this people has become dull, and with their ears they scarcely hear, and they have closed their eyes lest they should see with their eyes, and hear with their ears, and understand with their heart and return, and I should heal them. (Matthew 13:14-15)

The path to truth—God's truth—is hidden to many because only the Holy Spirit can reveal it. He is the only one who leads us into truth. If Christ is not a part of your life, Isaiah's prophesy applies to you.

If you have not become a "babe" and have not humbly called upon the Lord Jesus to forgive your sin and save your soul, you will not be able to find the path of life. Only those whose spiritual eyes have been opened by the Holy Spirit can see the path and find the treasure of His truth.

If you have not already done so, open your heart to Him today, that you too may find that path which leads to truth.

PART 1

GETTING OUR FEET WET

1

A Look at Biblical Paradoxes

". . .things which eye has not seen and ear has not heard, and which have not entered the heart of man, all that God has prepared for those who love Him." For to us God revealed them through the Spirit; for the Spirit searches all things, even the depths of God. For who among men knows the thoughts of a man except the spirit of the man, which is in him? Even so the thoughts of God no one knows except the Spirit of God. Now we have received, not the spirit of the world, but the Spirit who is from God, that we might know the things freely given to us by God, which things we also speak, not in words taught by human wisdom, but in those taught by the Spirit, combining spiritual thoughts with spiritual words. But a natural man does not accept the things of the Spirit of God; for they are foolishness to him, and he cannot understand them, because they are spiritually appraised. But he who is spiritual appraises all things, yet he himself is appraised by no man. For who has known the mind of the Lord, that he should instruct him? But we have the mind of Christ.

—1 Corinthians 2:9-16

My interest in biblical paradoxes came about, oddly enough, from a study of human communication. The word *communication* is derived from the Latin *communis,* which means "common."[1] Simply put,

---

1. *The American Heritage Dictionary of the English Language* (Boston: American Heritage and Houghton Mifflin, 1975).

it is the process whereby two individuals on the same wave length exchange and receive information.

However, it is often difficult for people to express what is "common" between them. Innuendos, half-expressed emotions, body language, symbolic gestures, and the baggage of culture make communication complex and often distort what the communicator is trying to say. Hence, a failure to master the art of communication can result in the deterioration of interpersonal relationships or even the breakup of a family.

In order to communicate with God, we need a common element to help us understand the content and intent of His revealed Word. That common element is the Holy Spirit. As the apostle Paul pointed out, without the work of the Holy Spirit, who intercedes for us even when we do not know how to communicate with God (Romans 8:26; 1 Corinthians 2:10-13), it is impossible to tie into God's wavelength. Thus believers, whom the Holy Spirit indwells, are the only ones who can understand God and who can be illuminated with His truth. Jesus clearly taught that when He declared of the majority of people who followed him, "Seeing they do not see, and while hearing they do not hear nor do they understand" (Matthew 13:13). The use of paradoxes in Scripture is a mighty demonstration of that principle.

A paradox, according to *Bakers Dictionary of Theology*, can be defined as "an assertion which contradicts some very commonly held position on the matter in question."[2] A paradox, then, is simply a seeming contradiction.

The following riddle provides a good illustration of a seeming contradiction.

> A father and his son go for an automobile ride. They are involved in an accident, and the father is killed. The boy, badly injured, is taken to the hospital for surgery. The doctor comes in, takes one look at the boy and says, "I can't operate on this boy, because he is my son." How can this be?

When I conduct seminars on the topic of communication, I like to use this riddle to demonstrate that preconceived perceptions many times keep us from properly interpreting what has been said. It is interesting to note that about 75 percent of any audience will fail to solve the riddle, even though the answer is quite obvious. Why? Be-

---

2. *Baker's Dictionary of Theology* (Grand Rapids: Baker, 1960).

cause there is an apparent contradiction: how can the father be dead and yet be alive to talk about his son? The seeming contradiction results because of a cultural mindset that expects physicians to be males. Thus we block out the possibility that it is the boy's mother who is the physician. When the computers in our minds do not allow us to see the obvious, we are forced to think of alternatives, which many times border on the ridiculous. So it is with biblical paradoxes. Our spiritual computers must be programmed by the designer Himself in order for us to comprehend, without any contradictions, the simple truth of a given passage.

When interpreting the paradoxical passages found in the Bible, the unbeliever has no other option than to misinterpret the intended meaning of God's Word. The believer, on the other hand, generally has two options. Either he finds himself repeatedly challenging deep-seated and highly respected cultural traditions that contradict biblical truth, or he chooses to ignore the Holy Spirit's message, becoming immune to the intended biblical message. By doing the latter he allows himself to be conformed to the world, to be squeezed into the mold and mindset of this present age.

There is no doubt that confronting cultural values and accepted practices calls for sacrifice. The price can sometimes be isolation and rejection, even from fellow believers. Compromise, on the other hand, although seeming to promote "good interpersonal relationships" and peer acceptance, may ultimately develop into a cancer that will eat away at our spiritual growth and our sensitivity to God's leading and direction. Such was the case with the Pharisees, who outwardly did everything right, yet could not communicate with God because their hearts were miles away from Him. Condemning the Pharisees for that, Christ said, "But in vain do they worship Me, teaching as doctrines the precepts of men. Neglecting the commandment of God, you hold to the tradition of men. . . . You nicely set aside the commandment of God in order to keep your tradition" (Mark 7: 7-9).

As a Christian sociologist I have observed that far too many of God's people are eager to view life through the eyes of the culture in which they find themselves. Those Christians may not have intentionally sought to live in direct opposition to biblical standards, but they have been subtly led by their environment to accept and even embrace the status quo. Many popular American values have led believers to be "conformed to this world" (Romans 12:1-2) to the degree that their lifestyles and values have contradicted God's pattern for their lives. This pattern is revealed to a large extent through the great paradoxes found in Scripture.

As a preface to our study of biblical paradoxes, two questions need to be asked: (1) What kinds of paradoxes exist in Scripture and how should they be interpreted? and, (2) Why does God use paradoxes to reveal His will?

There are basically two types of paradoxes found in the Bible: (1) those intended for doctrinal enlightenment (e.g., Jesus' discourse with Nicodemus concerning the paradox of spiritual rebirth; the paradox of the Trinity; and the paradox of God's sovereignty and man's responsibility), and (2) those intended to guide the believer in his life-style, in his interpersonal relationships, and in his attitudes. This book zeros in on the second group, seeking to answer the question, How do I, as a believer, view and respond to the world around me?

As we begin our study, our cornerstone will be the knowledge that truth is rational and comprehensible to the believer controlled by the Holy Spirit. One truth, then, cannot contradict other truths, and we will see that any seeming contradictions generally result from a conflict with cultural norms of accepted or expected behavior.[3]

From each paradox we will study, God intends us to derive one truth or primary meaning. That truth does not change from generation to generation.

Let us now consider the second question, Why does God use paradoxes to reveal His will? He does so to confound the "wise" of this world (1 Corinthians 1:27) and to draw His "sheep" to Himself (John 10:16). God uses paradox as a means of conveying His wisdom to the believer. To see how this selectivity of message functions, consider the idioms of language. If we were to go to a South American country, for example, and ask for a hamburger, we might receive a ham sandwich. However, anyone in tune with American eating immediately realizes that we mean a ground beef sandwich. The message of the paradoxes comes in a similar way. The intended meaning can only be understood by the believer who is in tune with God. Our thought patterns as Christians must be on a different wavelength, a higher plane than that of worldly logic and wisdom. The unbeliever, being blind to spiritual things because his ways are controlled by Satan (Ephesians 2:2), looks on a Scriptural paradox in frustrated or derisive bewilderment. A. W. Tozer described that bewilderment in the following way.

A real Christian is an odd number anyway. He feels supreme love

---

3. Eugene Nida, *Customs and Cultures* (New York: Harper & Row, 1954), pp. 49-52.

for one whom he has never seen. He talks familiarly every day to someone he cannot see, expects to go to heaven on virtue of another, empties himself in order that he might be full, admits he is wrong so he can be declared right, goes down in order to get up. He is strongest when he is weakest, richest when he is poorest, and happiest when he feels worst. He dies so he can live, forsakes in order to have, gives away so he can keep, sees the invisible, hears the inaudible, and knows that which passeth knowledge.[4]

As oil and water do not mix, so God's thoughts and ways can not be made compatible with the ways of the world (Isaiah 55:8). Down through the ages Satan has attempted through the "wisdom" of this world to separate man from God's truth and to convince man that he does not need the truth of God. He accomplishes that through the value systems and norms of existing culture (1 Corinthians 2:4-10).

It is imperative, then, that we believers not succumb to cultural thought patterns but so saturate ourselves in God's Word that we find no seeming contradictions, not only when studying, but also when applying the paradoxes of Scripture. It is in the application of truth that we must be aware of the enemy's tactics. Satan rejoices to see a discrepancy between God's truth and our behavior.

In our study of paradoxes, we will compare God's unchanging truth with current popular thought, using God's Word as a microscope to reveal the destructive cancer hidden in the world's view. The conclusions we draw will aid us in aligning our value system to the truth of Scripture.

---

4. A. W. Tozer, "Description of a Christian," *Good News Broadcaster* 28, no. 6 (June 1970), p. 11. The *Good News Broadcaster* is published in Lincoln, Nebraska.

STUDY QUESTIONS

1. In what ways does our culture challenge biblical truths?
2. State some ways in which compromise can stunt spiritual growth.
3. If one is not a Christian, he cannot understand God. Why, then, does God use paradoxes, which make understanding even more difficult?
4. Why does God choose to use paradox to reveal His will to the believer? Refer to the following passages: Isaiah 55:8; Romans 12:1-2; 1 Corinthians 2:4-7; 3:19; 12:14; 2 Corinthians 4:4; Colossians 1:9; James 1:5; 3:17.

PART 2

IN THE WORLD BUT NOT OF THE WORLD

2

Foolishness Brings Wisdom

Let no man deceive himself. If any man among you thinks
that he is wise in this age, let him become foolish, that he
may become wise.

—1 Corinthians 3:18

At no other time in history has the social pressure to receive an
education been so strong. Thirty years ago a high school diploma was
considered an accomplishment. Today a student must obtain a college degree in order to receive the same praise.

Although the accumulation of knowledge and wisdom has always
been a highly prized goal in refined and developed societies, Scripture teaches that earthly wisdom is condemned by God as foolish (1
Corinthians 1:20). Does this mean that all scientific findings and logical conclusions are in error? Obviously not. The problem, Scripturally
speaking, is not with the accumulation of knowledge, but with the inability of the human spirit to comprehend spiritual truth via natural
means.

First Corinthians 1:20-31 sets the stage:

20. Where is the wise man? Where is the scribe? Where is the de-
bater of this age? Has not God made foolish the wisdom of the
world?
21. For since in the wisdom of God the world through its wisdom
did not come to know God, God was well-pleased through the
foolishness of the message preached to save those who believe.

22. For indeed Jews ask for signs, and Greeks search for wisdom;
23. but we preach Christ crucified, to Jews a stumbling block, and to Gentiles, foolishness,
24. but to those who are the called, both Jews and Greeks, Christ the power of God and the wisdom of God.
25. Because the foolishness of God is wiser than men, and the weakness of God is stronger than men.
26. For consider your calling, brethren, that there were not many wise according to the flesh, not many noble;
27. but God has chosen the foolish things of the world to shame the wise, and God has chosen the weak things of the world to shame the things which are strong,
28. And the base things of the world and the despised, God has chosen, the things that are not, that He might nullify the things that are,
29. that no man should boast before God.
30. But by His doing you are in Christ Jesus, who became to us wisdom from God, and righteousness and sanctification, and redemption,
31. that, just as it is written, "let him who boasts, boast in the Lord."

BACKGROUND TO THE PARADOX

To fully understand the context of the above passage, it is important to observe two characteristics of the Corinthian life-style during Paul's day. First, the city of Corinth was a large and wealthy business seaport that included a mixed population of Romans, Jews, and Greeks. It also had the reputation of being a wicked, frivolous, and immoral city. Second, Corinth was noted for its centers of learning. It was known as the intellectual hub of the Roman Empire in Asia Minor. Paul even alluded to that in his epistle to the Corinthians, noting their drive for wisdom and eloquence of speech. It was like having Yale, Stanford, and Harvard all in the same city.

THE HEART OF THE MESSAGE

First Corinthians was written to the believers residing in that city. We are told that the spiritual state of the church in Corinth was "carnal," meaning that the believers' lives were governed by many worldly attitudes. Their thought patterns came from the world around them. The word *carnal* in the Greek means "fleshly," that is, in opposition to God's directives.

In referring to those in the church as "babes in Christ" (3:1), Paul is using a gentle touch of irony. Although addressing well-educated individuals, he uses the word "babes" to describe the condition of their spiritual maturity. Thus, the book is mainly written for exhortation, as a father would exhort his son, earnestly and in the spirit of love.

Because the Greeks were proud of their learning, Paul begins by contrasting earthly wisdom with heavenly wisdom. Earthly wisdom may be defined as an assimilation of knowledge that can be used or expressed in a rational manner. It implies good judgment and common sense.

On the surface that type of wisdom seems perfectly acceptable to us. However, it must be remembered that earthly wisdom uses human experiences as its foundation. In other words, if enough people say that black is white, or that what was right twenty years ago is not necessarily right today, then truth or reality becomes subject to change. Here, then, lies the difference between earthly wisdom and heavenly wisdom. Heavenly wisdom, the principles and absolutes of God's Word, are true regardless of whether five or five million give them credence.

Psychologist Solomon Asch conducted an interesting experiment designed to discover whether individuals will follow the majority even when the majority's judgment appears to be grossly deficient. The details of his interesting study are as follows:

> The basic Asch experiment involved one true subject, and six subjects who, unknown to the true subject, were actually confederates of the experimenter. They were presented with a vertical line of a certain length and were asked to match this line to one of three other lines of differing lengths. The answers were given aloud by one subject at a time. For the first few trials all the subjects were in agreement. But one of the confederates soon gave an answer which was clearly wrong, and the other confederates followed suit. Asch wanted to see if the real subject would conform or preserve an independent judgment in the face of this unanimous wrong verdict. The results? Between 30-40% of all true subjects conformed![1]

May we insert here a reflective question? What will happen if Christianity is someday considered irrational and belief in it is legal justification for incarceration in a mental hospital, as it is in Russia? Any society that bases its wisdom solely on human observation and logic is a prime candidate for such action.

1. Clifford T. Morgan, *Introduction to Psychology,* 5th ed. (New York: McGraw-Hill, 1975) pp. 406-7.

THE CYCLE OF EARTHLY WISDOM

God chose to make it impossible for man to come to know Him via earthly wisdom (v. 21). Why is it impossible? Let me describe the cycle earthly wisdom always takes. When earthly wisdom is sought as an end in itself, a false security develops because man trusts in that wisdom to guide him. That false security and trust become the basis for what we today would term humanism, which teaches that man can and should be in control of his own destiny. There are several times in Scripture where we see such a pattern developing. Interestingly enough, in the final phase of the cycle, we see God intervening with judgment. Here are three examples from the pages of Scripture.

(1) The Corinthian culture:
  a. The population of Romans, Jews, and Greeks represented an accumulation of knowledge from all of the existing known world.
  b. That knowledge led them to trust in their wisdom.
  c. God eventually intervened, for history indicates that during the fall of the Roman empire the Corinthian culture crumbled also.
(2) The description of the Tower of Babel found in Genesis 11:1-9. Note the comparisons:
  a. A conglomerate of different groups of people communicating in the samelanguage (v. 1).
  b. That oneness led to security (vv. 3-4), which turned into power as man appeared to have increasingly more control.
  c. God intervened, creating many languages and thwarting man's designs (vv. 7-9).
(3) The parable of the foolish rich man in Luke 12:16-21:
  a. In verses 16-18 we see the shrewd planning of human wisdom (a mindset based on the security obtained from riches).
  b. That allowed the rich man to trust in his riches (v. 19).
  c. God once again intervened (v. 20).

It is to be hoped that we will not have to add our own country as the fourth example. We have accumulated more wealth and technology in a shorter period of time than ever before. As a culture we prize self-help, independence, and self-sufficiency instead of God as the great "I Am" and the Lord Jesus as our only hope of salvation. We have fallen into the old trap of believing that we can do anything we set our minds to and that "where there is a will, there is a way." We have deified self and humanized God. We have neglected the primary condition for wisdom—the fear of God. We may look at Israel's repeated tumbles into apostasy in the Old Testament and why they couldn't seem to learn from their mistakes, while we ourselves continue in the very patterns we are warned against. First Corinthians 10:12 states, "Let him who thinks he stands take heed lest he fall."

CONTRASTING EARTHLY WISDOM TO HEAVENLY WISDOM

Scripture gives us eight distinctives to help clarify the differences between earthly wisdom and heavenly wisdom.

LOGIC AND REASONING

Earthly wisdom is derived from the senses, and human logic is based on past experiences. Spiritual wisdom is not always in tune with human logic or reasoning.

Earthly wisdom is validated by human consensus (1 Corinthians 1:22). Consider a recurring example from the Old Testament. Countless times Israel sought to make military pacts and alliances with other nations even though God specifically told them to believe He was all the protection they needed. They could not. Their earthly wisdom demanded false security and ignored the true security they could have had in their great Conqueror.

An example from the New Testament is Christ's resurrection. By the standards of earthly wisdom it was not logical and, therefore, could not be accepted. That was why Thomas had trouble believing that Christ actually had risen from the dead (John 20:24-29). He wanted proof positive (truth validated by his senses, in this case touch) that Jesus indeed had risen. His requirement was to put his hands in the nail-scarred hands and feet of Jesus and to observe the sword-pierced side. Some of us, while belittling Thomas's attitude on one hand, will on the other hand test God by using "fleeces" to ascertain His will. Either course reveals a faith that relies on experience for validation. Christ's response to such an attitude is, "Blessed are they who did not see, and yet believed" (John 20:29).

Spiritual wisdom, however, as manifested in the person of Jesus Christ (1 Corinthians 1:23), is not subject to human logic or reasoning (v. 18). I counseled a woman recently whose unbelieving husband had been involved in an affair. Today's society affirms that it is her right to obtain a divorce. Bev, however, chose to ask God to restore the joy that was lost in her marriage. Her marriage is not yet completely healed, but her faith, joy, and love have matured as she relies on the wisdom of 1 Corinthians 7:13: "And a woman who has an unbelieving husband, and he consent to live with her, let her not send her husband away." Because Bev's husband did not leave her, God's directive to her is to remain with him. In a narcissistic, over-indulging, and self-centered culture where the divorce rate increases rapidly every year, staying with an unfaithful partner does not appear to be a wise thing to do. Nevertheless, it is God's desire.

Additional passages to note: John 20: 24-29; Romans 8:26; Ephesians 3:18-19; Revelation 21:16.

DEPTH OF WISDOM

Earthly wisdom is only skin deep. In contrast, spiritual wisdom is able to penetrate the heart.

Isaiah the prophet wrote these penetrating words: "Then the Lord said . . . this people draw near with their words and honor Me with their lip service, but they remove their hearts from Me, and their reverence for Me consists of tradition learned by rote" (Isaiah 29:13). Earthly wisdom often results in legalism. That was the problem of the Pharisees. They surpassed what was required on the outside, but on the inside their hearts were far from God. Paul tells the Colossians,

> If you have died with Christ to the elementary principles of the world, why, as if you were living in the world, do you submit yourself to decrees, such as, "Do not handle, do not taste, do not touch!" (which all refer to things destined to perish with the using)—in accordance with the commandments and teachings of men? These are matters which have, to be sure, the appearance of wisdom in self-made religion and self-abasement and severe treatment of the body, but are of no value against fleshly indulgence. (Colossians 2:20-23)

Many cults demand conformity to set standards of dos and don'ts, and, unfortunately, some groups of true believers do as well. That may set a group apart outwardly, just as circumcision did for the Jews. But it cannot change the attitude of the heart.

Spiritual wisdom is able to penetrate the heart. Hebrews 4:12 tells us that "the Word of God is living and active and sharper than any two-edged sword." The spiritual wisdom that results as we establish our footsteps in God's word (Psalm 119:33) can cut through the masks we wear. It allows us to act out of a true conscience from a depth of being that is in tune with God's leading.

Additional passages to note: Isaiah 29:13-15; Luke 11:37-54.

THE EXAMPLE TO BE FOLLOWED

Earthly wisdom follows human example. Spiritual wisdom follows Christ's example.

Christ taught His disciples, "Let them [the Pharisees] alone; they are blind guides of the blind. And if a blind man guides a blind man, both will fall into a pit" (Matthew 15:14). The history of Israel shows that the leaders determined the spiritual course of the people. For when a king "did that what was evil in God's eyes," the people followed suit. And when the king pleased God, the people pleased God. The first chapter in the book of Habakkuk gives us a clear picture of the ease with which the Israelites followed the earthly wisdom of their wicked leaders: "The law is ignored and justice is never upheld. For the wicked surround the righteous; therefore justice comes out perverted" (Habakkuk 1:4).

The word *perverted* means "to give a wrong meaning to," or "to turn from the truth." The wicked king Jehoiakim led the people in perverting the truth. He brought Jewish society to the point of accepting wrong as right and black as white. Interestingly enough, the prophet Jeremiah, under the direction of the Holy Spirit, uses the same word to describe Israel's sin: "For you will no longer remember the oracle of the Lord, because every man's own word will become the oracle, and you have perverted the words of the living God, the Lord of hosts, our God" (Jeremiah 23:36).

The prophet Habakkuk describes the essence of true wisdom when he says, "The righteous will live by faith" (Habakkuk 2:4), and in 3:17-19,

> Though the fig tree should not blossom, and there be no fruit on the vines, though the yield of the olive should fail, and the fields produce no food, though the flock should be cut off from the fold, and there be no cattle in the stalls, yet I will exult in the Lord, I will rejoice in the God of my salvation. The Lord God is my strength, and He has made my feet like hinds feet, and makes me walk on my high places.

No matter what might happen, Habakkuk knew where his source and foundation and strength lay. His eyes were on God.

Today, true wisdom for believers is based on following Christ. In Colossians 2:2-3 Paul speaks of "Christ Himself, in whom are hidden all the treasures of wisdom and knowledge." That is why we are told in Philippians 2:5 to have the "mind of Christ." And in 1 Peter 2:21 we are admonished to "follow in His steps." Thus Spiritual wisdom is not concerned with how we feel or with what everyone else is doing, but rather with acting and relying on the principles we know to be right. Even if we do not at first feel like loving our enemy, as we allow Christ's Spirit to control and direct us our response will be filled with His wisdom and love.

Additional passages to note: Matthew 15:14; Romans 1:32; Colossians 2:8-10.

WHOSE ORDERS TO TAKE

Earthly wisdom is in tune with Satan's directives; spiritual wisdom is in tune with God's directives.

When Christ summed up the spiritual state of the Pharisees, He said, "You are of your father the devil, and you want to do the desires of your father. He was a murderer from the beginning, and does not stand in the truth, because there is no truth in him. Whenever he speaks a lie, he speaks from his own nature; for he is a liar, and the father of lies" (John 8:44). One thing we can note here: if a person is not a true believer, he cannot follow true wisdom because that privilege is reserved only for Christians. A nonbeliever is only capable of following the logic and reasoning of the world. Ultimately that logic is a lie, and its father is Satan.

Spiritual wisdom, however, is in tune with God's directives: "He who is of God hears the words of God; for this reason you do not hear them, because you are not of God" (John 8:47). Thus, to be able to understand the wisdom of God and make it part of us, we must truly be His children.

The apostle John echoed this thought when he wrote,

> We know that no one who is born of God [practices sin]; but He who was born of God keeps him and the evil one does not touch him. We know that we are of God, and the whole world lies in the power of the evil one. And we know that the Son of God has come, and has given us understanding, in order that we might know Him who is true, and we are in Him who is true, in His Son Jesus Christ. This is the true God and eternal life. (1 John 5:18-20)

Additional passages to note: Ephesians 2:2; Colossians 3:2.

WORSHIPING THE CREATOR AND NOT CREATION

Earthly wisdom worships the creation. Spiritual wisdom worships the Creator.

The apostle Paul wrote, "For they [the unrighteous] exchanged the truth of God for a lie, and worshiped and served the creature [nature] rather than the Creator, who is blessed for ever (Romans 1:25). A good Christian friend, Lowell Caneday, is professor of leisure studies at a well-known university. He has stated that we live in a culture that is geared toward worshiping creation rather than the Creator. Dr. Caneday believes the current "back to nature" emphasis is basically non-Christian. He has said, "In Scripture, every reference to the wilderness pictures spiritual drought, a place to avoid, not a euphoric place to desire. Many people feel the only way to get close to God is to meditate out in nature. What I fear, is that nature is taking pre-eminence over the Creator."[2]

An interesting parallel can be made to primitive cultures. In many of those societies, animal worship is practiced. We may term that a primitive practice, but a careful look reveals that it is not so different from the "back to nature" wisdom of the civilized world. Others may not choose the "back to nature" route, but instead will bow at the shrine of technology and science, material prosperity, or the arts. And even though the sports car or computer may replace the deer as an object of awe and desirability, the ramifications are the same. When the creation becomes the focal point of man, then man has exchanged the truth of God for a lie and serves what he has made. God the Creator is a spirit, and we must worship Him in spirit and in truth. Nothing we are able to know through our senses can portray the holy essence of the Ancient of Days. In God's Word, His Spirit reaches out to us. In prayer, our spirit finds the hand of the eternal Father.

Additional passages to note: Romans 12:1-2; Romans 1:17-25; Hebrews 11:25; John 3:16-18.

NOT IN STRENGTH BUT IN WEAKNESS

Flair and clout are vital to earthly wisdom. Humility and human

2. Dr. Lowell Caneday is currently chairman of the Leisure Studies Division at Oklahoma State University. He is a consultant for various governmental projects and is in demand as a speaker on the "back to nature" issue.

weakness are used by God to demonstrate spiritual wisdom. Jesus goes to the core of this issue when He says in John 7:18, "He who speaks from himself seeks his own glory; but He who is seeking the glory of the one who sent Him, He is true, and there is no unrighteousness in Him." Following the same vein of thought, Jesus spoke these words to His disciples:

> And when you pray, you are not to be as the hypocrites; for they love to stand and pray in the synagogues and on the street corners, in order to be seen by men. Truly I say to you, they have their reward in full.... And when you are praying, do not use meaningless repetition, as the Gentiles do, for they suppose that they will be heard for their many words. (Matthew 6:5, 7)

This, then, is the reward of a worldly-wise man—verbal praise and adoration from others.

Paul's statement that "God has chosen the weak things of the world to shame the things which are strong" (1 Corinthians 1:27) tells the Christian that humility and human weakness are used by God to demonstrate spiritual wisdom. The Greek word translated "weak" in this verse means "feeble, impotent." Why does God choose to work through weakness? He does so not because there is any virtue in being weak, but rather because human weakness magnifies His strength. Humility magnifies His glory. Proverbs 11:2 declares, "When pride comes, then comes dishonor, but with the humble is wisdom."

Additional passages to note: 1 Peter 5:5-6; Philippians 2:3-11.

CONTENTMENT RATHER THAN FUTILITY

The end result of worldly wisdom is futility. The end result of spiritual wisdom is contentment.

Solomon concluded toward the end of his life that "there is grief in much wisdom" (Ecclesiastes 1:18). And in Psalm 94:11 David says the "Lord knows that the thoughts of man are vanity." The word *vanity* in the Hebrew means "soap bubbles." Worldly wisdom ultimately will be as worthwhile as soap bubbles. Consequently, the vacuum it creates leads to anxiety and stress. Our society does not cope well with that stress. Some of the statistics are staggering: each year in America $295 million is spent on tranquilizers and $195 million on sleeping pills; 286 million gallons of hard liquor are consumed—at a yearly economic loss of $17 billion! A psychologist friend from a conservative East Texas county recently told me that there is enough Valium sold in that county to provide every man, woman, and child with one valium pill for every day of the year! Regardless of the advances man makes because of his wisdom, apart from God all of it becomes as futile as the soap bubble that vanishes into the air and is gone. "There is a way which seems right to a man, but its end is the way of death" (Proverbs 16:25).

On the other hand, spiritual wisdom, as it is followed by obedience, can be characterized by contentment and the ability to cope with stress. Peace instead of stress will be manifested if Christians follow the principles God has prescribed for positive spiritual and emotional health. "Casting all your anxiety upon Him, because He cares for you" (1 Peter 5:7) is more than a formula. It involves the totality of our inner selves reaching out to Him, and His promise in John 14:27 is the result: "My peace I give to you."

This mindset is totally foreign to the wisdom of this world. Many spend great amounts of time and money insulating themselves against the real and imagined fears of life. But as believers we are able to rest secure in God's love because His perfect love casts out fear (1 John 4:18). Therefore, we need not be anxious for anything. For as we commit ourselves to the principles of Philippians 4:6-9, the peace of God will guard our hearts and minds. Spiritual wisdom is not just rhetoric but a total belief in and commitment to the Christ who controls our circumstance.

Additional passages to note: 1 Timothy 6:6-11; Titus 1:15-16; 1 John 3: 24.

THE PURPOSE OF WISDOM

Earthly wisdom glories in self accomplishment, wealth, and wisdom itself. Spiritual wisdom glories in being able to know and understand God.

The prophet Jeremiah stated:

> Thus says the Lord, "Let not a wise man boast of his wisdom, and let not the mighty man boast of his might, let not a rich man boast of his riches; but let him who boasts boast of this, that he understands and knows Me, that I am the Lord who exercises loving kindness, justice and righteousness on earth; for I delight in these things," declares the Lord. (Jeremiah 9:23-24)

Down through the ages pride has been the Achilles's tendon of many people. And Christians unfortunately are not immune to the destruction pride can bring to a life. That insidious and subtle weakness may ultimately negate many of our "spiritual accomplishments" in the eyes of God.

Our actions might appear noble to men, but if the motive behind them is pride, we will exchange our eternal reward for a pile of wood, hay, and stubble. In our society a person's self image is wrapped up in what he does and how well he can do it. We begin to compare and rank each other as early as preschool days. Life takes on the appearance of a series of ladders, with each step up the rungs bringing more self-confidence and egotistic pride. After being immersed in those doctrines from childhood, many believers find it a great spiritual struggle to gain release from that mold and to begin patterning their thinking according to what Christ says in John 15:5, "Apart from Me you can do nothing."

To allow Christ to give life meaning and purpose, to do what we do for His glory, to rejoice not in our accomplishments but rather in knowing Him is a freedom the world cannot know or understand.

Additional passages to note: 1 Corinthians 1:29-31; 1 Corinthians 2:1-5.

Putting Wisdom in Its Proper Light

At the outset we proposed that scientific findings and logical conclusions are incomplete in their ability to reach the essence of truth. Looking for that essence, we have contrasted earthly wisdom to heavenly wisdom. In summary, we have made some distinct differences between the two—differences the Christian can use to assess his growth toward true spiritual wisdom.

Earthly Wisdom	Heavenly Wisdom
No standard of authority	The final authority of all wisdom is the word of God
Assumes the intrinsic goodness of man	Assumes the true sinfulness of man
Anthropocentric (man based)	Theocentric (God based)
Goal: Self-acceptance, self-actualization, for self-happiness, self-health, and a safe society	Goal: The whole development of the whole man, reflecting the whole image of God, to the whole glory of God

Finally, it can be said that all truth is from God. That includes the wisdom gained by secular thinkers and researchers as well as the truth proclaimed in the Scriptures. However, because the Bible is the final authority for all truth, it is the standard and criterion by which all knowledge is tested. Data in accord with biblical revelation should be considered valid and should be integrated into one's world and life view. On the other hand, data contradicted by the Scriptures should be regarded as invalid and therefore must be rejected as non-truth or unwise. Here are two verses that can help us make this distinction:

> Beloved, do not believe every spirit, but test the spirits to see whether they are from God; because many false prophets have gone out into the world. (1 John 4:1)

> Be diligent to present yourself approved to God as a workman who does not need to be ashamed, handling accurately the word of truth. (2 Timothy 2:15)

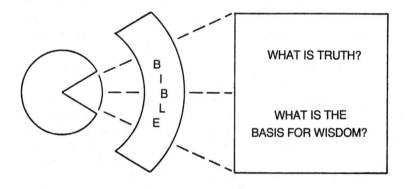

"WISDOM": A BRIEF WORD STUDY

In the Old Testament the word *wisdom* is used approximately 150 times, with over half of those references found in the Wisdom literature (Job, Proverbs, and Ecclesiastes). Those references outside Wisdom literature seldom refer to God, or even spiritual wisdom, but rather to human skills or abilities that may or may not be specially God-given. In the Wisdom literature, *wisdom* often refers merely to humanly derived knowledge (Ecclesiastes 1:13; Job 4:21), which brings only grief and frustration (Ecclesiastes 1:12; 2:9-11). In contrast with human wisdom, however, there is divine wisdom, given by God and enabling man to lead a good and true and satisfying life.

The Old Testament concept of divine wisdom must not be abstracted from its practical implications for men. The truly wise man is the good man, and the truly good man is he who at the very beginning wisely chooses to give God the proper place in his life (Psalm 111:10).

The New Testament adds the distinctive element of wisdom's identification with Jesus Christ (1 Corinthians 1:24). Some of the usages of wisdom in the New Testament include: wisdom as a divine attribute of God (Luke 11:49); its revelation of the divine will to man (1 Corinthians 2:4-7); its nature as the spiritual understanding of God's will for man (Matthew 13:54; James 1:5); wisdom as a capacity of the human intellect (Matthew 11:25; 12:42); and the possibility that pride in human wisdom can lead to destruction (1 Corinthians 1:19-20).

What is wisdom? Synonyms include: understanding, good paths, discretion, good sense, truth, excellent things, right things, prudence, counsel, strength, common sense, good judgment, life, and happiness. According to Webster, wisdom is the ability to judge soundly and to deal sagaciously with facts, especially as they relate to life and conduct. Harry A. Ironside says that wisdom is not so much holding the truth as being held by it. Someone else has said that wisdom is the ability to understand an end, and the means of achieving that end, and the performance of those means. And another that whereas knowledge is a basic truth, wisdom is that truth in action (e.g., Proverbs 14:4; 26; 31). Wisdom is the wedding of knowing and doing, the junction of the good and the true. You can have knowledge without wisdom. But you can't have wisdom without knowledge. The Bible often talks of wisdom as if it were a person (e.g., Proverbs 8, esp. vv. 20-36; Matthew 11:19; 1 Corinthians 1:24). It also proclaims that the fear of God is wisdom (e.g., Psalm 111:10; Proverbs 1:7).

The Scriptures leave no question that wisdom is something to be desired. Wisdom is desirable because it is our only guard against evil (Proverbs 1:5-7, 23; 3:23, 35; 4:6, 8-9; 5:2; 9:1-2). It is necessary in order to avoid eating the fruit of our own way (see 1:24-33). Wisdom is the way to live a fulfilled life in happiness (3:4, 13-18; 8:10-11, 18-21; 24:3-5, 13-19). We must *not* desire wisdom because we think it would put God in our debt (Proverbs 9:10-12).

There is a warning, an exhortation to the saved and to the unsaved to—"wise-up" 1:24-33.

How do we get wisdom? First of all, by dwelling in the Word of God (Proverbs 2:1-6; 5:1-2; 8:17). Second, we must simply choose it. All we need to know in order to have wisdom is there for the taking. It will probably mean changing so that we live an orderly and disciplined life of obedience (3:19-23; 4:10-13, 25; 8:1-3, 32-34; 9:3-6, 10). Third, wisdom can be gained through adopting the postures of wisdom (trust, humility, and wholeheartedness) and its aspects (generosity and submission, see 3:5-12). Fourth, we get wisdom simply by asking for it (James 1:5).

The results of wisdom include discernment (Proverbs 1:2; 16:21; 22:9), truth (1:3), knowledge (2:10 ff; 8:12; 13:16; 15:2, 7; 18:15; 19:25; 28:2, 6), happiness (3:13), discretion (8:12; 13:10; 19:11), and good judgment (8:15; 16:20; 17:2; 24:23).

Seven building blocks for developing a godly strategy for life may be discerned (see the *Living Bible* for clarity). The wise man is one who (1) thinks ahead (Proverbs 13:16); (2) adjusts to a changing world (13:19); (3) faces the facts (14:18); (4) utilizes the counsel of others (15:22); (5) realizes God is in control (16:1); (6) plans well (18:13); and (7) is always open to new ideas (18:16).

HUMANISTIC AND BIBLICAL THINKING

Following earthly wisdom will lead to a humanistic outlook on life. That term is often used by the church today to represent anything that is evil. From a simplistic view, secular humanism deifies man, humanizes God, and legalizes sin. The particulars of secular humanism, however, need to be pointed out so the Christian can accurately battle its philosophy and influence.

Secular humanism, which by the way has been declared by the United States Supreme Court to be a religion, adheres to the following points: (1) The mind of man is the key to a better world. Reason and intelligence are the most effective instruments that mankind possesses; (2) Happiness on this earth is all men can hope for because there is no supreme God, no heaven, and no life after death; (3) There is no such thing as an absolute. All behavior is relative. Thus all acts are morally neutral; (4) Morals are derived from human experience only. Religion is thus a product of culture; (5) Humanism adheres to the existential philosophy of "do your own thing"; (6) Man, in essence, becomes a god to himself. He thus sees himself as the master of his own destiny.[3]

3. For an excellent overview of the subject of humanism, refer to Nancy Barcus, "The Humanist Builds His House on the Sand," *Moody Monthly* 81, no. 1 (September 1980) pp. 24-30.

The anti-humanist position bases its source of wisdom on fearing God and living a life that is holy. Verses to support that view include: Psalm 111:10; Proverbs 2:2-5; 15:33; and Jeremiah 5:22; 15:19.

When the fear of the Lord becomes a reality in our lives, He will give us the ability (wisdom) to extract the meaningful from the worthless, He will allow us to be His spokesman, and He will grant us the privilege of helping others do the same.

1. It was pointed out that our country is succumbing to the notion of self-sufficiency. What attitudes and actions ought Christians take to combat this trend?

2. Many times we read Scripture and say, "Why didn't Israel repent and turn back to God, especially when God performed so many miracles to prove His power?" It seems as though every culture fails God and has to pay the consequences. Why do we not learn from the past, knowing that what we sow we will reap?

3. It was brought out that earthly wisdom worships the creation instead of the Creator. Because of this, to what extent should we be involved in the ecology movement?

4. What does humanism mean to you? Is it a real threat to your life, or is it merely a philosophical position? Discuss.

5. Take a few minutes to find various verses from the book of Proverbs concerning wisdom. Go around the room and share a verse and tell what it says about true wisdom and how we are to apply it to our daily lives.

3

Dwelling Below
While Seated Above

But God, being rich in mercy, because of His great love with
which He loved us, even when we were dead in our trans-
gressions, made us alive together with Christ (by grace you
have been saved), and raised us up with Him, and seated us
with Him in the heavenly places, in Christ Jesus . . . So then
you are no longer strangers and aliens, but you are fellow citizens with the saints, and are of God's household.

—Ephesians 2:4-6, 19

THE CHRISTIAN'S SOURCE OF SECURITY

Insecurity. Of all the fears that people face, the inability to obtain a
warranty on life, whether it be in the realm of the material or the
emotional, ranks as one of the major threats to an individual's peace
of mind.[1] And it is interesting that Scripture indicates the world's
compelling drive for security is similar to grasping for a mirage, a desire that can never be guaranteed or satisfied.

However, Christians have a security from God more real than any
the world has to offer. In the midst of the natural insecurities of life,
we have an oasis—a fertile green spot—in a desert of waste. This benefit we enjoy as Christians of "being seated with Him in the heavenly

---

1. James C. Coleman, *Contemporary Psychology and Effective Behavior,* 4th ed.
(Glenview, Ill.: Scott, Foresman, 1974), pp. 100-104.

places" begins the very moment we become alive in Him. We are
now seated with Him in the heavenly places, even though we dwell
here below. Concerning the opening passage, Kenneth Wuest states,

> "Hath raised us up together" relates to life now, in a present spiritu-
> al sense. The [Greek word] expresses the definite idea of resurrec-
> tion, and primarily that of physical resurrection. In Paul's mind, he
> did not sharply distinguish between the present moral resurrection
> and that of the future bodily resurrection, but thought of them as
> one great gift of life.
>
> "Seated us with Him in the heavenlies" [can be interpreted] that
> He has made us sharers with Him in dignity and dominion, so that
> even now, and in foretaste of our future exaltation, our life and
> thought are raised to the heavenlies where He reigns.[2]

I grasped a clearer understanding of this paradox while traveling
through Indonesia several years ago. My group was scheduled to go
into the interior of Irian Jaya, but as all Indonesian missionaries are
aware, the gateway to Irian Jaya is through the capital city, Jakarta.
Most will agree that Jakarta is not one of the cleanest, safest, or most
hospitable places in the world. In the center of this city, however, sits
the Christian and Missionary Alliance guest house called IMBO (Inner
Mission Business Office). IMBO not only serves as a guest house, but
the director also arranges all the paperwork for those traveling to Irian Jaya, picks up people from the airport, makes sure all needs are
met—the list goes on and on.

Trying to make it without the IMBO staff would indeed have been
quite difficult for us. Even though we were newcomers to that part of
the world, we experienced a sense of security and peace of mind because of their assistance. We also were comforted in the fact that
there were other missionaries staying at the guest house. Here we
were, halfway around the world, yet we were comfortable and secure
because we were able to communicate from both a cultural and spiritual perspective with the new friends we had made. We no longer
had the feeling of being a stranger or an alien because we were
among friends, "seated" with fellow citizens in a wonderful oasis.

In the same way, we as believers are at rest in the oasis of God's
promises and love. We no longer need to try to find security and
peace in an inhospitable world. And because we "have been raised up

2. Kenneth Wuest, *Wuest's Word Studies from the Greek New Testament*, vol. 1,
Notes on Ephesians (Grand Rapids: Eerdmans, 1966), pp. 67-68.

with Christ" (Colossians 3:1), we naturally begin to seek the things that are above, "where Christ is."

THE CHRISTIAN AS A "MARGINAL" PERSON

Our minds and hearts naturally gravitate to causes of the King and His kingdom; herein is our peace and joy and security. However, we are still residents of the earth, and that is our Father's will. But what earthly lifestyle best reflects the dual role of being seated above while dwelling below? First, the reality that we have already become seated above in the heavenlies should provide us with the security needed to operate in an insecure world. And second, we have what I call *marginality*, the mindset we need to operate in this world.

Dwelling below while seated above is a call to a marginal status in life. Sociologists use the term to describe a person who exists on the peripheral or outside rim of a culture. A person of marginal status in many ways does not fit in anywhere and finds that no matter where he is, he is not quite at home.

A missionary is a good example of this principle. He never expects to become fully assimilated into the culture of the country where he ministers.[3] Yet, after a period of years, the same missionary finds it difficult to readapt to his own culture, because he has been changed and influenced by his experiences as a missionary. His experiences in both cultures have made him a marginal person. He doesn't "fit" anywhere.

In similar fashion, once we become Christians, we find ourselves in the world but no longer of it. The call to marginalization is the intended meaning of Romans 12:1-2, which admonishes us not to "be conformed to this world, but be transformed by the renewing of your mind." Or as the Phillips translation puts it, "Don't let the world around you squeeze you into its mold."

After we are saved, we must never again get so wrapped up in the things of this world that we fail to enjoy or even seek the things above, where Christ is seated. As we obey the admonition of Colossians 3:2 to "set your mind on the things above, not on the things that are on earth," marginalization is the natural result. We are no longer bound by the desires and attitudes that bind the rest of society. We begin to seriously assess the difference between what we actually need and what society says we need. We are willing to accept the la-

3. See John E. Conklin, *An Introduction to Sociology* (New York: Macmillan, 1984), pp. 204-5.

bel of oddball or fanatic as we hunger more and more for things of eternal value.

THE PULL OF SOCIETY

To adequately understand marginalization, or life on the edge of culture, we must be aware of the vulnerabilities of such a life as well as the advantages. We can accomplish that best as we come to appreciate what sociologists call the *acculturation* process.[4]

Acculturation is the process each of us undergoes whereby we are made part and parcel of our particular society. More than we can ever be aware, our culture shapes the way we feel about things, our traditions, our likes and dislikes, our values—attitudes that ultimately become our behaviors. For example, what we deem appropriate in terms of dress or modesty is culturally determined. In Irian Jaya, many of the Ok Bap males feel immodest if they are not wearing their gourd. In our culture, however, the definition of modesty is different.

Another area in the acculturation process is the type of food a particular group of people accepts and enjoys. I recall several years ago seeing a newspaper picture of a person in Bangladesh eating rat meat. My stomach turned over just looking at it, and probably I was not alone! However, in the culture of Bangladesh, rat meat is a delicacy. And, unless the rat is infected, the nutritional value would not be any less than our beef. Yet we would never consider taking one bite, unless on the verge of starvation. Why? Because we have grown up with a particular mindset that refuses to accept rat meat as acceptable food. The bottom line of acculturation then is this: we not only learn a way of doing things and a way of thinking—we also learn that that way is the right way.

As we become acculturated we develop a *cultural identity*. This basically establishes us as "in" with a particular group, and everyone who is different is "out" and, to a certain extent, is treated accordingly. Generally speaking, anyone who has not been acculturated in this way is seen as a stranger or, worse yet, an oddball. For psychological reasons, then, there is a definite need for acculturation—for identity, for security, and for self-esteem. These, then, become the payoffs for belonging to a society.

---

4. Philip K. Bock, *Modern Cultural Anthropology* (New York: Alfred A. Knopf, 1974), pp. 225-26.

IDENTITY

Identity has many aspects, including the national, professional, racial, ethnic, physical, and religious. All of those parts of a person's identity are integrated in a cultural context so that who an individual is quite literally becomes a product of acculturation. Being a part of a culture ensures someone that he will know who he is, where he belongs, and what his jobs, benefits, and relationships are to be. This is the identity the world offers.

SECURITY

Security is knowing what to expect in any given situation. Social customs, protocol, manners, and the like are all ways that individuals become secure in their surroundings. Insecurity produces anxiety. In my counseling I have sometimes seen the children of expatriates and missionaries develop anxieties because they must learn to function in two cultures. (Generally, however, once the children learn to handle their duo-cultural role they tend to be even more stable than their single-cultural counterparts.)

SELF-ESTEEM

Having had the experience of living and traveling in other countries, I am still surprised to realize how vulnerable my self-esteem can become when I am out of my home territory. The jobs I perform and the positions I hold set the parameters for my identity. And when I get out of a certain setting, I can see the props collapse. I am aware of other people who have had this same experience. So our own constituency gives us a sense of self-esteem and importance—of worth as an individual.

These, then, are the benefits of acculturation. The question that naturally emerges is, What happens then when we as Christians move to the margin or outskirts of a culture? To be quite frank, in a very real and human sense it means giving up all the benefits of acculturation. That is the price that must be paid for "living below, yet seated above."

COPING WITH MARGINALITY

No matter how glorious and exciting our lives are after we become saved, each of us must deal with the price we pay for a marginal life. There are at least four ways Christians deal with marginalization. The first three can create problems.

FORCING OTHERS TO CONFORM TO US

The first one is to make everybody else like us. This is in social and psychological terms what colonialism was in political terms. The result of forcing Christian values on people who are not believers produces a society where there is outward adherence to Christian values but inward rejection of Christ. This was the problem when Constantine converted to Christianity and forced all of the Roman empire to do likewise. The "church" that resulted perfectly fit Christ's characterization in Matthew 15:8-9: "This people honors Me with their lips, but their heart is far away from Me. But in vain do they worship Me, teaching as doctrines the precepts of men." Forcing change, as Constantine tried to do, is 180 degrees apart in scope and philosophy from true Christian principles.

CONFORMING TO OTHERS

The second approach to marginalization is compromise with a culture. In other words, "If you can't beat them, join them." Rationalizing one portion of Scripture and then another, we continually inch back toward that comfortable center of culture. We excuse our actions with the words "If we're too different, we'll never be able to win anybody to the Lord. We've got to go with the times." Many individuals and denominations have accepted this way of thinking. The Bible teaches, however, that we are to come out from the world and be separate.

ISOLATING OURSELVES

The third response is the isolation approach. "OK, if I have to live at the margin, I will erect walls so that the vast majority of my experiences, work, education, friends, and acquaintances will occur within my safe, closed community." As a result, a we-they mentality is developed in order to keep those boundaries sharp and clear. A close look at Christ's life, however, reveals that He did not accept this approach. This lifestyle really has its roots in the attitude of the Pharisees, who accused Jesus of being a drunkard and associating with non-desirables. The apostle Paul in 1 Corinthians 5:11-13 also tells us that in order to win the lost for Christ, we must associate with those of the world.

FULLY EMBRACING MARGINALIZATION

The fourth response, and the one I believe to be the most accurate approach, is a joyful submission to the call of marginalization. Knowledgeable acceptance of our call to be seated above while we dwell below will eliminate many of the struggles we might otherwise face while trying to fit into the mainstream of our culture or become isolated from it. It will also make it easier to understand Christ's words without becoming threatened: "If the world hates you, you know that it has hated Me before it hated you. If you were of the world, the world would love its own; but because you are not of the world, but I chose you out of the world, therefore the world hates you" (John 15: 18-19).

As we live on the margin of culture, the apostle Peter says "Pass the time of your sojourning here in fear" (1 Peter 1:17, KJV*). Sojourning is a state of non-permanance. The essence of marginalization is not being an outcast but rather a traveler. Hence we are not to become too comfortable, because we really are not home.

Kenneth Wuest adds,

> The word "sojourning" is from a word meaning literally "to have a home along side" and refers to a person's living in a foreign land among people who are not his kind. Here it refers to children of God living far from their heavenly home. The Christian must always live in the consciousness of the fact that he is being watched by the unsaved, that his responsibility is to bear a clear, ringing, genuine testimony to His God and Saviour by the kind of life he lives.[5]

Similarly, David states, "Lord . . . let me know how transient I am" (Psalm 39:4). The Christian position is one of apartness, of being marginal, of not quite belonging to this world system. Jesus did not quite belong, as John records: "He came unto His own, and those who were His own did not receive Him" (John 1:11). And once we effectively learn to live on the outskirts of culture, we will conclude that the security the world has to offer is fleeting at best, that traditional norms have become suspect, and that our old values, which entrenched us in vanity, will no longer motivate us.[6]

* King James Version.
5. Kenneth Wuest, *Wuest's Word Studies from the Greek New Testament*, vol. 2, *Notes on I Peter* (Grand Rapids: Eerdmans, 1966), p. 41.
6. D. Stuart Briscoe, *When the Going Gets Tough* (Ventura, Calif.: Regal, 1982), pp. 63-64.

The dedicated Christian realizes that marginal status in relation to the world is the price to be paid for being a follower of God. As a result, he will always be exposed and vulnerable. While dwelling here below, he will not experience the security the world offers but will know the greater peace and security of being seated above, already participating in eternal joys.

ADAPTING TO A MARGINAL LIFE-STYLE

If we as Christians are called to a marginal life-style, how are we to adapt to the status of being marginal? Fortunately, God never asks us to do anything without first supplying the necessary tools and equipment.

First, in order to effectively adapt to marginal living we must have a heart knowledge that we are citizens of heaven. The apostle Paul tells us, "For our citizenship is in heaven, from which also we eagerly wait for a Savior, the Lord Jesus Christ" (Philippians 3:20). A heart knowledge of this fact will make us yearn for that day when the transition Christ has begun in our lives will be complete, and we will be with Him forever (Philippians 1:6). (See chapter 12.)

Second, we must be genuinely and deeply convinced that as we move to the margin of culture we are there because Christ is Lord, and He has called us there. As I flip through the hymn book, I am somewhat dismayed to find songs that approach the Christian life from a negative point of view, songs declaring that nobody seems to care about our plight as suffering Christians, that our labor goes unrewarded, and so on. True, we may be unrewarded in terms of the way in which the world views rewards, but in terms of eternal gains—those that are most real—we will never lack! When we feel buffeted or enticed by the world, we must always come back to our call—our reason for being there on the edge. Things will be lost in terms of our acculturation to a particular society, but in terms of spiritual gains, rewards will be accumulated. We must come back to that calling then when we are buffeted by the changes of marginal living.

Third, and most important from a practical standpoint, we must find at the margin of culture a new community. The community is the church, the Body of Christ. The church is the Christian's home away from home. We are set apart and not well received by the world, and in a sense we are homeless. The church becomes our community, our identity, and our security. The Body of Christ is, in a real way, a society—it is the divine society.

Fourth, to survive on the margin of culture we need to operate our life in the framework of God's peace, peace that is supplied to those Christians who live in tune to God's leading and follow His principles. Several times in Philippians 4 the peace of God is mentioned. It is promised when certain requirements are fulfilled, such as actively choosing not to worry, maintaining a faithful prayer life, rejoicing in all things, and keeping a pure thought life. Once we have done those things, Paul says, "The things you have learned and received and heard and seen in me, practice these things; and the God of peace shall be with you" (Philippians 4:9). The capstone is verse 13, which reads "I can do all things through Him who strengthens me."

The Benefits of Marginality

Why does God call us to a marginal life? We are not there just because we are iconoclasts or because we enjoy punishment or a lack of security. We are there because Christ is Lord, and He has called us. Yes, we are called out from the world to be transformed into the image of Christ Himself as we pointed out in Romans 12:1-2. In fact, the more like Christ we become, the closer we will find we are to that margin, that edge. Another way of saying it is that the pathway to spiritual maturity is the path that leads from the center of the world's culture and system out toward the edge, as we press on toward the mark of the our high calling in Christ Jesus.

Yes, by living on the margin Christians can expect to lose some identity, security, and self-esteem, as the world defines those terms. But Christ gives us more of an identity and security than the world can ever offer, because He allows us to be joint heirs with Him in glory.

To be seated above while dwelling below, then, involves a commitment to live life on the margin of culture. To do so is to be truly alive and vital as Jesus Christ was and is.

STUDY QUESTIONS

1. We are a "peculiar people" (1 Peter 2:9, KJV). Does this mean Christians are to be ten years behind the times in terms of dress style and so on?
2. How have you experienced marginalization? How have you dealt with this issue?
3. What are some ways we can keep in perspective the fact that our citizenship is in heaven?
4. In what ways does the Body of Christ, the church, function as a community or society?
5. Comment on the statement that "spiritual maturity is the pathway from the core of the world system to the outskirts of that system."

4

The One Shall Become Two— The Paradox of Our Times

And some Pharisees came up to to Him, testing Him, and began to question Him whether it was lawful for a man to divorce a wife. And He answered and said to them, "What did Moses command you?" And they said, "Moses permitted a man to write a certificate of divorce and send her away." But Jesus said to them, "Because of your hardness of heart he wrote you this commandment. But from the beginning of creation, God made them male and female. For this cause a man shall leave his father and mother, and the two shall become one flesh; consequently they are no longer two, but one flesh. What therefore God has joined together, let no man separate. And in the house the disciples began questioning Him about this again. And He said to them, "Whoever divorces his wife and marries another woman commits adultery against her; and if she herself divorces her husband and marries another man, she is committing adultery."

—Mark 10:2-12

Only the one-shall-become-two paradox is an exception to the others, for to accept and practice it leads away from truth and God. Yet it is vital that we understand that Satan has used this paradox to blur and confuse us. Through it, he has turned the sharp, clear focus of the truth of God's Word into a fuzzy, rosy distortion. Too many of us prefer that colorful, fuzzy, soft distortion to the piercing, precise words Christ speaks to the Pharisees in Mark 10.

The biblical principles that became the basis of the traditional nuclear family (one lifetime marriage, husband principal breadwinner, several children) have been replaced by a variety of arrangements. People (many Christians included) have come to view their intimate arrangements as a matter of personal, rather than public, concern. Pluralism and privacy are strong themes in today's intimate relationships. As a result, the family as it has been known is changing; in several areas of the United States it is almost obsolete. A complicated and often confusing pattern is emerging for the institution of the family.

Assuming that the social changes predicted in the next fifty years do occur, *U.S. News and World Report* made this sad commentary on the typical family of the future.

> One spring afternoon half a century from today the Joneses may gather to sing "Happy Birthday" to Junior.
>
> There is Dad and his third wife, Mom and her second husband, Junior's two half brothers from his father's first marriage, his six stepsisters from his mother's spouses's previous unions, 100 year-old Great-Grandpa, all eight of Junior's current "grandparents," assorted aunts, uncles-in-law and stepcousins.
>
> While one robot scoops up the gift wrappings, and another blows out the candles, Junior makes a wish . . . that he didn't have so many relatives.[1]

Experts say that over the next five decades society will redefine its concept of the family. Through the pattern of divorce and remarriage, a whole new network of kinship is developing. The ability to relate to one another and commit to one another on anything beyond a surface level is vanishing. Though we still mouth the words "the two shall become one," our easy acceptance of divorce has made "one shall become two" the real truth.

One Dallas family court judge was recently quoted as saying, "It's a sign of the times. Marriage used to be a three-way contract between a husband, a wife, and God. Now, if they see something that looks more interesting, there they go." Consequently, our throw-away culture

---

1. "When the Family Will Have a New Definition," *U.S. News and World Report,* 9 May 1983.

dispenses with a broken-down marriage as easily as it discards a broken-down TV or washing machine.

CHANGING ATTITUDES TOWARD DIVORCE

My files are full of accumulated articles on how society treats the divorce issue and the effects of divorce, even among Christians. Here are some examples:

• We can now subscribe to a periodical entitled *Journal of Divorce*. This magazine is proud that it "continues to be the authoritative and timely resource that covers in depth all aspects of divorce."

• "The divorce rate increased 96% during the last decade," states one article. It also points out that the census report indicated an "increasing percentage of unmarried men and women are living together."[2]

• "Divorce Insurance Seen" is the title of another newspaper article that states, "Today you don't walk into a marriage without realizing that it could be broken up."[3]

• "Anita Bryant now has milder views on homosexuality" headlines a Sunday newspaper. "She's now more inclined to say 'live and let live' as long as sexual preference is kept in the closet."[4] Does divorce lead to further compromise of values?

• In a report entitled, "Divorce now so commonplace it's an asset in business world," Virginia Payette says:

> Divorce has become a way of life, something that happens sooner or later to half the marriages in the country. Didn't we, for the first time in history, elect a president who's been divorced? Not only did we, but it was such a ho-hum incident in his past that not even the Democrats bothered to mention it against him.
>
> According to a survey by the National Personnel Association, 61 percent of the 237 personnel agencies they interviewed said divorced job-hunters are "hot candidates" for management positions.
>
> A male applicant gets snapped up because the boss figures he's all his, and is more available for transfers.
>
> A woman with children is "highly prized" because she needs the

2. "Divorce Rate Increases 96% over Decade," UPI release, *Longview Daily News* (Longview, Texas), 2 April 1980.
3. "Divorce Insurance Seen," UPI release, *Longview Daily News*, 8 August 1979.
4. "Anita Bryant Now Has Milder Views on Homosexuality," AP release, *Longview Daily News*, 16 November 1980.

money and will probably be willing to work harder for less pay.[5]

• Divorce loans are now available. A Dallas firm now offers this service.

• Dallas and Houston are tied for the highest divorce rate in the country. Why? According to one researcher, divorce results from mobility, a highly competitive society, a decline in church attendance, separate careers, a rich social environment, and relaxed laws that make divorce relatively simple.[6]

• "It took just 20 minutes and a few words from a judge to make 108 people believers in lawyer Averil Sweitzer's proud claim to be the leading undoer of marriages in Dallas," a news article reported.[7]

• George W. Cornell, an Associated Press religion writer, states, "Divorce, which used to be virtually non-existent among the clergy, has become increasingly common, and to some extent, more accepted by church-goers."[8]

• A Florida firm now advertises a "Divorce Kit." The advertisement claims to be the "first and leading publishers and mailorder distributors of copyrighted do-it-yourself divorce forms for Florida" (cost: $20).

• A couple is reported to have returned to the altar where they were married to rescind their vows in a divorce ceremony. The pastor said, "Divorce is the only major life trauma for which the church has no ritual." Portions of one such ceremony went like this:

> The Pastor: The two of you once stood in a place like this before God, and exchanged vows of commitment in marriage. Those vows were made in good faith. But sometimes even the most earnest vows cannot be kept.
>
> The Wife: Dave, I release you as my husband and ask you to be my friend. I cannot be your wife, but I affirm again my love and respect for you.
>
> The Pastor: I declare that you are, before God, released from your bonds of marriage and are no longer husband and wife. You are set

5. Virginia Payette, "Divorce Now So Commonplace, It's an Asset in Business World," United Feature Syndicate release, *Longview Daily News,* 1 January 1981.
6. Leslie Pound, "Dallas Life Brings Divorce After 32 Years," New York Times News Service release, *Longview Daily News,* 30 April 1982.
7. "Mass Divorce 'Unmarries' 108," AP release, *Longview Daily News,* 21 August 1983.
8. "Clergy Divorces More Common, Still a Problem," AP release, *Longview Daily News,* 27 March 1982.

> free to face new futures as separate persons. Carry no burden of
> guilt or recrimination for what is past.[9]

I looked for the husband's response, but it was not given. What
caught my attention was the pastor's statement, "Carry no burden of
guilt for what is past." Some believe a mere declaration by a pastor
can alleviate the guilt and sin of a divorce!

As a counselor, I am saddened by all the material written by "evangelical" authors that seems to minimize what Jesus said on the subject
of divorce. I am convinced that their cut-and-paste approach to the
subject is no different from the existential "do my own thing" philosophy that permeates our society today. I see the effect of that philosophy quite often in the Christians I counsel. Such a philosophy lets
us act the way we want and then pull a few Bible verses out of context to vindicate and justify our behavior. Our approach is backward.
Our goal should be to fit our behavior to the whole counsel of Scripture, instead of trying to squeeze a meaning out of Scripture to fit our
desires. We ought never forget that "God is not mocked; for whatever
a man sows, this he will also reap"(Galatians 6:7).

THE RESULTS OF DIVORCE

We cannot deny that there are untold ramifications to a divorce.
That is another black-and-white truth that Satan would like us to see
through rose-colored glasses. But even non-Christian psychologists
and sociologists cannnot overlook what divorce and remarriage is doing to our culture.

• Divorce and its stress lead to many health problems. One study
showed that the death rate from heart disease is two to three times
higher for divorced women than for married women. The report
went on to state that divorce has also been linked to asthma, rheuma-
toid arthritis, hyperthyroidism, genital herpes, ulcers, colitis, yeast infections, disruption of the menstrual cycle, headaches, and depression. Why? According to Dr. Kathryn Kramer, director of corporate
health services at St. Louis Medical Center, "Major life events like divorce signal a rapid, abrupt change in a person's orientation."[10]

• Parental divorce creates difficulties for young adults. Studies now

---

9. "Ceremony Eases Pain of Divorce," AP release, *Longview Daily News,* 16 September 1980.
10. "Divorce and Its Stress Lead to Many Health Problems," *Cosmopolitan,* released to
Longview Daily News, 3 December 1984.

show that divorce drastically affects many children, even after they are grown and have left home.[11]

• Divorce threatens the futures of children. In a study conducted by the American Academy of Child Psychiatry, it was reported that "divorce can be so traumatic for young children that they become adults who are psychologically incapable of leading happy lives."[12]

• It has now been determined that adolescent daughters of divorced parents tend to be more uninhibited, overly active, aggressive, and flirtatious compared to adolescent girls coming from a home where the father has died.[13]

• Children's books now have a whole new category—how to cope with the divorce of their parents. Titles include, *Now I Have a Stepparent, The Kids Book of Divorce, My Friend Has Four Parents,* and *Where Do I Belong.* Isn't it a shame that this type of material needs to be written? I would classify the harm done to children through divorce to be as damaging as child abuse; but in a society that insists on individuality, the problem is simply looked upon as a social inconvenience.

WHY IS DIVORCE WRONG?

Most Christians will agree that divorce is wrong, but many will qualify that position in one way or another. Because of the rampant escalation of divorce in our society, many who formerly did not accept even the thought of divorce are now accommodating the practice —and usually remarriage goes hand in hand with divorce. It is important, therefore, to consider the biblical reasons that divorce is wrong and should not be considered an option by a couple.

First, according to Ephesians 5 a Christian marriage is the visible symbol of the invisible relationship we have with Jesus Christ. A destruction of the marriage union reflects poorly on our Christian witness to an unsaved world.

Second, for many people divorce means giving in to "the lust of the flesh, the lust of the eyes, and the boastful pride of life" (1 John 2:16). A psychologist has told me that one evangelical church he was aware of has a divorced group of approximately one hundred, 60-70 per-

11. Andree Brooks, "Parental Divorce Creates Difficulties," NY Times News Service, *Longview Daily News,* 2 December 1984.
12. "Divorce Threatens Kids' Future, A Study Says," AP release, *Longview Daily News,* 6 November 1983.
13. John W. Santrock, *Adolescence, an Introduction,* 2d ed. (Dubuque, Iowa: William C. Brown, 1984), p. 262.

cent of whom led active sex lives following their divorces. It seems that for most people, once they have chosen to divorce, choosing to fornicate becomes fairly easy. And each step in the process takes them further from God.

Third, divorce causes man to blaspheme against God. God says, "I hate divorce" (Malachi 2:16), but man rationalizes that actually God does not really mean it and that his or her situation is different—and the exception to the rule.

Fourth, divorce has negative effects on the family—not just the children, but the extended family as well.

Fifth, divorce reflects and accepts hardness of heart (Jeremiah 3:8; Mark 10:4).

Sixth, 1 Corinthians 6 states that Christians are to solve their problems in the local church and not in the public courts. Every Christian marriage that ends up in the divorce court gives another reason for non-Christians to belittle our faith and our Lord.

And, seventh, divorce ought not be an option for the Christian because it forces one to break a vow that was made to a spouse and to God. Solomon put it so well when he wrote:

> When you make a vow to God, do not be late in paying it, for He takes no delight in fools. Pay what you vow! It is better that you should not vow than that you should vow and not pay. Do not let your speech cause you to sin and do not say in the presence of the messenger of God that it was a mistake. Why should God be angry on account of your voice and destroy the work of your hands? For in many dreams and in many words there is emptiness. Rather, fear God. (Ecclesiastes 5:4-7)

Our marriage vows are declared in the presence of God and are as much a covenant with God as they are with our spouses. Breaking a covenant vow is serious business to God, and His righteous anger is kindled against churches who treat His Word so lightly that they have actually instituted divorce ceremonies.

But let us say you have already become part of that ever increasing number of divorced Christians. My experience in counseling has proved to me over and over that even though God will graciously forgive the truly repentant sinner, the consequence and effect of that sin cannot be completely erased.

In Psalm 103 David rejoices in God's total cleansing and forgiveness of his sin with Bathsheba. He knew God had pardoned him (v.

3), had put away His anger from him (v. 9), had removed the
transgression from him (v. 12), and had lovingkindness and compassion toward him (vv. 11, 13). God *can* and *will* wash away our guilt.
Nonetheless, the *consequences* of David's sin remained with him
throughout his life. The infant Bathsheba bore him died, and there
was distress and rebellion in his own household from then on, just as
Nathan the prophet predicted (2 Samuel 12:10-11). One of God's
spiritual "laws" is found in Galatians 6:7-8. We *will* reap what we
have sown.

Does this mean then that those who have already divorced can
have no spiritual victory, joy, or blessing? Absolutely not. Once the
sin is confessed and repented of, the way is open for God's renewed
work in the believer's life. Even though the handicaps and the consequences of the sin remain, God's renewed blessing can give joy and
victory in all things.

And the next question that naturally arises is, what about the Body
of Christ? What should our attitude be toward those who are divorced? Perhaps much like Samuel's when Israel rejected God's rule
and asked for a king. Samuel declared that he would continue to up-
hold them in prayer before the Lord and to serve them with the gift
God had given him (1 Samuel 12:23-24). This should be our attitude
as part of the Body of Christ. We love, we support, we serve, and we
pray for one another, in humility, gentleness, and true biblical
wisdom.

THE CHRISTIAN FAMILY, A UNIQUE SPECIES

The evangelical view on divorce has not changed overnight. It has
changed gradually and insidiously over the past twenty years. That is
one of Satan's easiest tricks. Christians are analogous to the frog in the
pan of water. Biologists tell us that if a frog is placed in a pot of boiling
water, it will immediately jump out. But if that frog is placed in a pot
of lukewarm water and the heat is turned up gradually, the frog will
simply sit and boil to death. So it is with our doctrinal stance on marriage. The theology that accomodates and minimizes divorce will
eventually kill many evangelical churches. And looking into the future, what area will next be attacked and a compromising resignation
be allowed to set in? In what area of our faith will we next accept the
lukewarm mediocrity so detestable to our God that it causes Him to
vomit in Holy revulsion (Revelation 3:14-19)?

Divorce occurs today because marriage is no longer based on a covenant relationship but rather on convenience. It is no longer based on God's absolutes and values that are subject to God's definition but rather on the shifting subjective values of man. Divorce occurs because the home is now characterized by selfish independence—"I have my rights, don't violate my territory"—rather than unselfish dependence, wherein we give up our rights to our spouse and God. And finally, marriage is becoming dualistic (two individuals who happen to live together) rather than monistic—where the two actually become one flesh.

Please, dear Christian brother or sister, do not allow yourself to become a player in the world's favorite game of rationalization. Instead of entertaining thoughts of divorce and fantasies of greener grass, determine before God to obey His Word and honor Him.

And even if the road ahead seems more than you can cope with, remember that God promises to reward and exalt those who humble themselves in obedience before Him. The eternal benefits of working to hang on to a marriage far outweigh any transient satisfaction the world's way can offer.

The Christian community is being attacked from within and without on this vital issue. Many are buckling under the pressure to conform to the world's system of thought.[14] It is up to us. What will it be: the two shall become one, or the one shall become two? Our children await our answer.

---

14. Roger C. Palms, "The Vow-Keepers," *Moody Monthly,* December 1984, pp.116-17. This article is one of the best I have seen dealing with the permanency of the marriage vow. I would strongly suggest your reading it. Another excellent book is J. Carl Laney, *The Divorce Myth, a Biblical Examination of Divorce and Remarriage* (Minneapolis: Bethany House, 1981).

STUDY QUESTIONS

1. The "theology of accommodation" was used in this chapter to explain how churches deal with the issue of divorce. In what other situations are Christians inclined to use this same theology?
2. Read the book of Hosea. Discuss why Hosea went out and bought back his prostitute wife. Does that incident provide an example for us?
3. Should churches have special Sunday school classes for divorcees? Discuss.
4. In what specific ways can the church (meaning the Body of Christ) help one who has already been divorced?
5. Should limitations in terms of church office positions be imposed on those who are divorced? Give reasons.

PART 3

WHERE THE RUBBER MEETS THE ROAD

5

Servitude Brings Greatness

> Whoever wishes to become great among you shall be your
> servant, and whoever wishes to be first among you shall be
> your slave; just as the Son of Man did not come to be served,
> but to serve, and to give His life a ransom for many.
>
> —Matthew 20:26-28

I have been involved in athletics all my life. I played basketball in
high school and college and coached that sport at the college level
for seven years. I have vivid memories of my coaches barking out
such statements as, "For you to be great, you must win!" "You've got
to learn to hate your opponent. The bottom line is winning!" and,
"Great things come to great winners."

That philosophy is not limited to the athletic world. Generally, the
attitudes displayed in the athletic world simply mirror those found in
society as a whole. The mindset that demands that we be the "top ba-
nana" no matter the cost is one that Americans have adopted whole-
heartedly in every area of life.

Our affluent culture forever bombards us with opportunities for
self-gratification. Rejection of the concept of servitude is epidemic in
our modern world. Why serve? Why be humble? Humility is un-
American. The Western value system calls for greatness, success, and
status regardless of who or what must be sacrificed. Consequently,
servanthood is looked upon as mere piousness, fit only for those living in monasteries.

And most alarming, that view of greatness has become the motivat-

ing force of many Christians. Such a motivation keeps believers carnal, cold, and unstable; and Christ's statement in Matthew 20 concerning servitude becomes mystical and quixotic instead of a vital
reality. Carnal Christians have fallen prey to the misconception that
one must strive hard to achieve greatness because his individual
worthiness is at stake. The believer who walks with God becomes
motivated by totally different desires and goals. His deepest love becomes the kingdom of his Lord, and his joy becomes serving, "because the goal in the kingdom is not to rule, but to serve."[1]

In John F. Walvoord's comments on Matthew 20:25-28 he explains
that Jesus "acknowledged that in worldly kingdoms, places of power
with great authority are sought. But He declared that in the kingdom
of heaven, it shall be different. The road to privileged authority is often paved with lowly service."[2]

By way of comparison, then, the natural or carnal man believes that
life's goal consists of elevating and magnifying self, with the payoff being influence and power—the ability to manipulate others even
though God says that type of greatness lasts but for a fleeting moment. The man led by the Spirit of God, however, believes that life's
goal consists of serving, which elevates and magnifies Christ, with the
payoff being true and lasting greatness in eternity.

REARRANGING OUR NOTIONS OF SERVITUDE AND GREATNESS

Because we as believers are to elevate and magnify Christ through
our servitude, perhaps we should spend some time discussing the
way in which certain common words carry different connotations in
Scripture from that generally given to them.

To begin with, the Holy Spirit saw fit to repeatedly use one phrase
(e.g., Matthew 19:30; 20:16; Mark 9:35; 10:31; Luke 13:30) in speaking of servitude and greatness: "But many who are first will be last;
and the last, first" (Matthew 19:30). Why is that phrase repeated so
many times? Is it because the Holy Spirit is striving to impress upon
us that no one can handle the awesome responsibilities of being first
in the kingdom until he is willing to be last? Merrill F. Unger adds
these thoughts:

> God does not evaluate man's service as man evaluates it. Some who
> are prominent and apparently successful in Christian work, whom

1. John F. Walvoord, *Matthew: Thy Kingdom Come* (Chicago, Moody, 1974), p. 151.
2. Ibid.

we look upon as greatly used by God, will appear near the bottom of the Lord's list of faithful servants, while humble, self-effacing servants, little recognized by men, will appear at the top. Moreover, we are to be interested in the Lord's service primarily, not in the reward; in the quality, not the length of service.[3]

True greatness and worthy ambition thus hinge directly on our motivation for service. Their manifestation is humility. The only reward desired is the Kingdom's furtherance and increase.

HUMILITY

Because humility is the manifestation of true greatness, it obviously should become the foundation for our attitudes and lifestyle. That will sound pretty ridiculous to most people today, who consider humility to be only a lack of pride.

The spiritual man's definition of humility differs 180 degrees. As Ronald Goetz points out,

> Biblical humility is not the inverted conceit which disguises itself as lowliness. It is that attitude which results from a fearlessly honest self-appraisal, a self-appraisal which neither minimizes one's achievements nor exaggerates ones failures. Humility is not the subtle masochism which enjoys its own debasement.[4]

Mr. Goetz tells us what humility is not. But what is it? It is total, unashamed, and open dependence upon God. It is being so motivated by our love for God and His creation that we do not even notice when we are wronged. It is loving when love is not returned. It is Christ's mind in us (Philippians 2).

Humility is unique to biblical faith and teaching. Other religions teach a masochistic self-debasement as a poor substitute. But only philosophers influenced by the Judeo-Christian tradition teach anything about its true form.[5] In Micah 6:8, for example, we are told that humility is a godly virtue. In the Old Testament we find that God's prophets were humble and were exalted by God even after their

---

3. Merrill F. Unger, *The New Unger's Bible Handbook*, rev. Gary N. Larson (Chicago, Moody, 1966, 1984), p.347.

4. Ronald Goetz, "Proud to Be Humble," *Christian Century* 96, no. 7, 28 February 1979, p. 207.

5. V. C. Grounds, *Zondervan Pictorial Encyclopedia of the Bible*, vol. 3 (Grand Rapids: Zondervan, 1975), p. 222.

deaths. In Numbers 12:3 we are told that Moses was the most humble man who ever lived, yet he was exalted and made leader of God's people. In the New Testament we find God Himself giving us the supreme example of humility by sending His son to earth in human form. He suffered the cross for our sins but then was exalted and will be made King over all the earth.[6]

Any believer who walks closely with God displays humility as a natural outgrowth of that relationship, because as he becomes more aware of his wonderful Lord and the perfect holiness of His being, he also becomes more aware of his own sinfulness and shortcomings.[7] So the key to humility is not self deprecation but close communion with the Lord.

GREATNESS

Jesus said, "You are those who justify yourselves in the sight of men, but God knows your hearts; for that which is highly esteemed among men is detestable in the sight of God" (Luke 16:15). What a warning for those of us who are Christians. If we seek greatness and esteem from men, we have detoured from God's track. Why is the world's definition of greatness an abomination to God? It is detestable because such greatness comes from the standards set by the prince of this world, Satan himself.

The true criteria for greatness seems foolishness to man, and man's standard is of no consequence to God. When Israel demanded a king, for example, God said to Samuel, "Do not look at his appearance or at the height of his stature, because I have rejected him; for God sees not as man sees, for man looks at the outward appearance, but the Lord looks at the heart" (1 Samuel 16:7). Because the natural man does not have the mind of God in him, his judgment on greatness can only relate to external observable criteria. However, the pride and ability to manipulate, which are ever a part of such criteria, are exactly those things that eventually will cause the natural man to fall. As Luke 14:11 declares, "For everyone who exalts himself shall be humbled, and he who humbles himself shall be exalted."

The spiritual man realizes that his heart and priorities must be attuned to Christ's directives. How is that done? By waiting on the Lord and allowing Him to do the exalting according to His own time and choosing: "Humble yourselves, therefore, under the mighty hand of

6. Goetz, p. 207.
7. Grounds, p. 223.

God, that He may exalt you at the proper time, casting all your anxiety upon Him, because He cares for you" (1 Peter 5:6-7). As we submit in obedience to verse 6, we are guaranteed in verse 7 a greater, deeper security and peace than any the world could ever hope to offer.

AMBITION

The way ambition is viewed is the third major difference between the perspective of the natural man and that of the spiritual man. As believers, should we view ambition as sinful? Consider these passages:

> Not that I speak from want, for I have learned to be content in whatever circumstances I am. I know how to get along with humble means, and I also know how to live in prosperity; in any and every circumstance I have learned the secret of being filled and going hungry, both of having abundance and suffering need. (Philippians 4:11-12)

> But godliness actually is a means of great gain, when accompanied by contentment. For we have brought nothing into the world, so we cannot take anything out of it either. And if we have food and covering, with these we shall be content. But those who want to get rich fall into temptation and a snare and many foolish and harmful desires which plunge men into ruin and destruction. For the love of money is a root of all sorts of evil, and some by longing for it have wandered away from the faith, and pierced themselves with many a pang. (1 Timothy 6:6-10)

Does that mean that if our old car is still running we should not seek a newer one? Does it mean that if we fail to get that raise at work we should not seek a job change?

Harry A. Ironside has brought some insight into that question. He believes that we are to act like a contented child, having full trust and peace in our heavenly Father.[8] Contentment here is not a call to a lifestyle similar to the caste system of India; rather, our contentment is based on a willing acceptance of the place or appointment given to us by God. Because of that Paul was able to say in Philippians 4:12 that he could be satisfied whether he be rich or poor.

The practical application of the message is this: We must have a

---

8. Harry A. Ironside, *Expository Notes on the Gospel of Matthew* (New York: Loizeaux Brothers, 1948), pp. 221-25.

willingness to take the lowest place in life (like many of the Old Testament prophets) if that is God's desire, or we must be willing to take the highest place in life (like David and Solomon) if that be God's will. And because of that, wherever God puts us we are to be ambitious there, so that we may win the race (1 Corinthians 9:24-27) when it really counts. If that is our philosophy, we will not need to compare ourselves to others—which is very much a part of ambition as defined by the world's mindset. God judges the Christian's ambition and performance in terms of faithfulness. The following provides a good example:

> Suppose you were to fill several different sized glasses with water. If you fill a pint glass, that is all it will hold. If you fill a quart jar, that is all it will hold. If you fill a gallon jug, that is all it will hold. Each one is given all it can hold. The pint is just as full as the gallon. By comparison, one is bigger than the other, but by experience each is full.[9]

When it comes to ambition, big and handsome places for ourselves ought not be our number-one priority (i.e., the gallon jug). Rather we are to seek only to do God's will on this earth, making sure our container, whatever size it may be, is full. If it is an obscure place God chooses for us, we can and ought to be happy in it and do our best by it. A total willingness to hold back nothing at the command of Christ should be our natural response to Him. So we are not to seek poverty or wealth, greatness or debasement. We are to seek only to do the will of our heavenly Father.

JESUS' TEACHING ON SERVITUDE AND GREATNESS FROM THE BOOK OF MATTHEW

To be spiritually and emotionally healthy as Christians, our lives must be under the total direction of the Holy Spirit. Compromising with the world will lead to frustration, disappointment, and confusion. In the message to Laodicea, God says, "I know your deeds, that you are neither cold or hot; I would that you were cold or hot. So because you are lukewarm, and neither cold or hot, I will spit you out of My mouth" (Revelation 3:15-16). Compromising with the world leads ultimately to a lukewarm state, and that is something God cannot tolerate. To remain true to God, to be "hot" for Him, requires that we embrace servitude as a way of life. Our greatest boast should echo

---

9. Manford G. Gutzke, *Plain Talk on Matthew* (Grand Rapids: Zondervan, 1977), p. 166.

the apostle Paul, who proclaimed himself to be a bondslave of the Lord Jesus.

Christ spoke often of servitude and greatness. I have chosen just six such instances from the book of Matthew in order to draw out important principles to conclude with. For each principle, a brief background, along with the message, the key idea, and the natural man's reaction to this teaching, will be presented. These six principles are presented in outline form in order to provide clarity and also to simplify the process of evaluation.

PRINCIPLE NUMBER 1

Passage: Matthew 13:31-32.

Background: Discourse to the disciples on the mysteries (or hidden truth) of the kingdom of heaven.

Message: Parable of the Mustard Seed (the least of seeds becomes the greatest).

Key idea: Greatness is externally, not internally initiated. If sown by Christ, the result is greatness. (Jesus says in John 15:16, "You did not choose Me, but I choose you.")

Natural man's reaction to this idea: From the world's point of view, greatness results from determination, shrewdness, discipline, and pride. Greatness is self-initiated, not externally initiated.

PRINCIPLE NUMBER 2

Passage: Matthew 16:24-25.

Background: Peter rebuked for his pride; Jesus' discourse on the cost of discipleship.

Message: To be a disciple, one must deny self (i.e., give up ownership). Christ must be number one, not I.

Key idea: To deny self does not mean we are to harm or deprive ourselves (many religions teach this), but we are to keep our priorities straight and our eyes on the things that really count.

Natural man's reaction to this idea: Self-exaltation is the key to success. We need to put ourselves on pedestals and work to be noticed in order to gain approval and commendation.

PRINCIPLE NUMBER 3

Passage: Matthew 18:1-4.

Background: Disciples arguing on the position of each in the Kingdom. They still thought at this time that Christ was going to set up an earthly kingdom in the near future. They wanted power, position and influence.

Message: Christ compares the qualities of a little child to greatness in the Kingdom.

Key ideas: When it comes to greatness, God shows no favoritism. Christ uses the child concept to emphasize the necessity to place our trust and dependency on the Father.

Natural man's reaction to these ideas: The world system is built on status and clout. In the world one cannot trust anyone but himself; if he does, he will be taken advantage of. Independence is valued; the goal is freedom.

PRINCIPLE NUMBER 4

Passage: Matthew 20:15-16.

Background: Christ's discourse to His disciples on God's sovereignty (v. 15). We do not set the rules; He does.

Message: The parable of the laborers in the vineyard: the employer paid all workers the same wage even though some had worked more hours.

Key ideas: The believer's earthly role is subject to Christ's desires. Christ gives out of His abundance as He sees fit, not according to human logic. True greatness is not dependent on length of time one has been a Christian. We are to work not for position but out of love.

Natural man's reaction to these ideas: One is responsible only to himself and his own desires. Rewards should be commensurate to length of service.

PRINCIPLE NUMBER 5

Passage: Matthew 20:20-24.

Background: When James and John did not make headway with Christ concerning the position they desired in the kingdom, their mother came to intercede for them.

Message: The price of greatness is suffering.

Key ideas: Ambition must be paralleled to heavenly directives. To be really great in God's eyes we must minister, serve, and obey no matter the cost.

Natural man's reaction to these ideas: Earthly success is the only reflection of ambition. (One company I am aware of boasts about its relationship to the "80-20" principle: 20 percent of the people make

80 percent of the wealth in this country, and its goal is to be a part of that 20 percent.) To be great, one must humble his subordinates. It is necessary to be in the limelight so that others will quickly notice your accomplishments.

PRINCIPLE NUMBER 6

Passage: Matthew 23:1-12.

Background: Christ characterizes the Pharisees and pronounces judgment on them (v. 13).

Message: The works done by the Pharisees were done to be seen by men and therefore bring glory to themselves.

Key idea: Service brings honor. Christ did not say we are to despise the gifts God has given us to use for His service. What He does mean is that we are not to serve in order to gain the admiration and praise of others. We serve to bring glory to God, as 1 Corinthians 1:31 points out: "Let him who boasts, boast in the Lord."

Natural man's reaction to this idea: Human praise builds and confirms one's ego. Self-identity and self-worth must be validated and measured by others.

BENEFITS FOR FOLLOWING CHRIST'S FORMULA FOR SERVITUDE

If we follow Christ's example to serve others, we will grow spiritually, and our testimony will be vibrant in the midst of a self-serving world. It is hard to paddle against the current, but if we do, true and lasting success and greatness will be our reward.

STUDY QUESTIONS

1. What are some practical guidelines that we can use to make sure our ambition is harnessed to God's desire and not the world's?
2. If we are to be humble, how can a person in business ever market his skills?
3. Summarize the six principles of servitude and greatness that Jesus presents in the book of Matthew. Identify those difficult areas that make it hard to follow His teaching because of the pressures of society.
4. In Matthew 20:20-24 Jesus points out that the price of greatness is suffering. Why do you suppose God has ordained that?
5. From the insights gained as a result of reading this chapter, identify three ways you can implement Christ's principles on humility and servitude at home and at work.

6

In Need, Yet Provided For

The Lord will not allow the righteous to hunger.

—Proverbs 10:3

I have been in labor and hardship, through many sleepless nights, in hunger and thirst, often without food, in cold and exposure.

—2 Corinthians 11:27

A few weeks ago I picked up a Christian periodical that devoted its entire issue to the famine-plagued areas of northeast Africa. One story described a father's plight as he sold his children into slavery in exchange for food. Another article zeroed in on the children starving in Ethiopia. A third talked about relief efforts by Christian organizations and made an appeal for a financial contribution to the plight of the needy in Africa. The pictures were shocking. The articles were explosive. And my initial reaction? One of guilt, one of sorrow, and one of introspection—realizing how much I waste here in comfortable America.

The ramifications of that explosive subject are mind-boggling. While discussing this issue with a friend who has served his life as a missionary in Africa, I asked him a question that had been more and more on my mind: "In light of all the specific Scripture promises to the contrary, is it still possible for a true Christian to starve to death?"

His reply was quite interesting. "Rick," he said, "you're on to one of your intellectual nonsense games again—like how many angels can sit on top of a needle. You should spend your time on more important and pragmatic issues that can benefit the cause of Christ."

Was my friend right? Is it an issue that is better left unanswered or untouched? I think not. Even though my friend dismissed the validity of the question, I concluded that the way we view the matter is indeed important, for our answers reflect our perception of God's sovereignty, how God relates to man, and how we are to serve Him in this world (i.e., mission strategy).

The Bible declares that God is in control of all that happens in this world. "As Christians, we are obligated to interrelate this sovereign view of God with present-day realities," states Walt Olsen, professor of Cross Cultural Studies, LeTourneau College. "We are to tackle problems faced in the real world, even this highly emotional famine issue, with confidence, and not be afraid to put Scripture to the test."

Pondering the issue of famine, one recurring question surfaces in my mind. Are any of these people who are suffering and dying brothers and sisters in Christ? What about the precious and familiar verses that promise God's provision in times of famine and plague:

> Behold, the eye of the Lord is on those who fear Him, on those who hope for His lovingkindness, to deliver their soul from death, and to keep them alive in famine. (Psalm 33:18-19)

> O fear the Lord, you His saints; for to those who fear Him, there is no want. The young lions do lack and suffer hunger; but they who seek the Lord shall not be in want of any good thing. (Psalm 34:9-10)

> In the days of famine they will have abundance. (Psalm 37:19)

> I have been young, and now I am old; yet I have not seen the righteous forsaken, or his descendants begging bread. (Psalm 37:25)

> He will have compassion on the poor and needy, and the lives of the needy he will save. (Psalm 72:13)

> They all wait for Thee, to give them their food in due season. (Psalm 104:27)

> For He has satisfied the thirsty soul, and the hungry soul He has filled with what is good. (Psalm 107:9)

He has given food to those who fear Him. (Psalm 111:5)

The Lord will not allow the righteous to hunger. (Proverbs 10:3)

He who walks righteously, and speaks with sincerity, he who rejects unjust gain, and shakes his hands so that they hold no bribe; he who stops his ears from hearing about bloodshed, and shuts his eyes from looking upon evil; he will dwell on the heights; his refuge will be the impregnable rock; his bread will be given him; his water will be sure. (Isaiah 33:15-16)

But seek first His kingdom and His righteousness; and all these things [food and raiment-v. 31] shall be added to you. (Matthew 6:33) [The same two items are mentioned in 1 Timothy 6:8]

Now He who supplies seed to the sower and bread for food, will supply and multiply your seed for sowing and increase the harvest of your righteousness. (2 Corinthians 9:10)

And my God shall supply all your needs according to His riches in glory in Christ Jesus. (Philippians 4:19)

How are we to interpret these passages? Do they contradict reality? We can read of God's promises for provision on the one hand, but on the other, we see vivid reminders of starvation in famine-plagued areas of the world, even among groups claiming to be Christian. What is the answer? How should we as evangelical Christians answer this perplexing question? From my research I have found four basic views.[1] (1) These promises can be taken literally and thus literally claimed by Christians today. (2) They ought to be viewed as guides for Christian behavior and attitude, realizing, however, that a sovereign God may alter a situation for His eternal purpose. (3) They are dispensational, with special meaning or reference for the nation of Israel. (4) These promises must be viewed from the social angle—that is, if Christians would do their part in helping their brothers or sisters in need, starvation would not be a concern.

---

1. I am grateful to those individuals who, either by telephone or by correspondence, allowed me to present their views on this subject of starvation. My intent at the outset was to poll those evangelicals who could be considered authorities to obtain their thinking on this critical issue. I was surprised to learn in the process that this question has not been addressed apart from the Christian responsibility to the poor.

THE PROMISES AS LITERAL

Scripture is full of many examples in which provision was given in time of need. Joseph was used by God to save his people from famine. Moses pleaded with God in the wilderness for food, and manna was sent; when water was needed, the rock opened up. The widow had just enough oil to last one more day, yet God made that oil go on and on. Elijah and Jesus were fed in the wilderness. And the list goes on.

"I believe there is no basis for a Christian who is obeying the commands of Christ to say he can die of starvation," states Jerry Borner, dean of Biblical Studies at CBN University. "There are just too many passages that are directly applicable to any righteous individual—Jew or Gentile."

Concurring with this line of thought, James Kennedy, pastor of the Coral Ridge Presbyterian Church in Fort Lauderdale, Florida, says, "The principle is this: Given any kind of economic situation, God will intervene to help the believer who is righteous and obedient in a way a nonbeliever cannot experience. If that be not the case, being righteous means nothing on this earth."

Dr. Kennedy goes on to clarify his position. "Both extremes of this issue are wrong. We can't say if I am righteous God will give me anything I want, Cadillac and all, nor can I say that God's promises are only for eternity. We can spiritualize 'give us this day our daily bread,' but for the one who is hungry, it can be claimed as a literal need. This may seem harsh to say, but how do we know if those who are dying of starvation in Ethiopia are truly obedient born again believers? Only God knows this."

"The bottom line is that the righteous man will not starve to death," claims Lowell Caneday, chairman of Leisure Science at Oklahoma State University and authority on natural resource productivity and outdoor education.

> The problem stems from an inability to see the question from God's perspective. In our human economy, we are told we cannot go over several days without water. But in the economy of God, we see examples of men going 40 days without food or water. I firmly believe God will provide our basic needs [not cultural needs] if we can operate in the framework of God's economy. For modern day examples of this principle, read the stories of Corrie ten Boom, George Mueller, and others who witnessed God's intervening when all earthly hope had vanished.

J. Dwight Pentecost, professor at Dallas Theological Seminary, who holds to this view, comments, "We need to remember the promises made in the Psalms and Proverbs cannot be claimed in their totality by Christians today. There may be, however, an indirect application or principle that can be made for the church in this dispensation. The context of these promises refers to the covenant God made with his chosen people."

Throughout the ages God has divinely ordered the events of this world. "The focus of God's plan and work," states Don Row, "has shifted from the Jews to the church in this current dispensation. In Leviticus 26, and Deuteronomy 28 for example, we are told of the conditional covenant made with Israel."

> If you walk in My statutes and keep My commandments so as to carry them out, then I shall give you rains in their season, so that the land will yield its produce and the trees of the field will bear their fruit. (Leviticus 26:3-4)

Summarizing this position, Dr. Pentecost concludes, "We are not promised relief from suffering, hunger included. We will suffer because we live in an unredeemed world. It is within God's power to provide, but He is not bound to do so. It may very well be His will to test us with hunger as a means of witness for Him."

As a footnote, Dr. Pentecost also believes that the Matthew 6 passage that promises food and clothing if we seek His kingdom and His righteousness refers primarily to the millennial reign of Christ. But, as mentioned before, even though that promise cannot be literally claimed in this dispensation, we can rest in God's sovereign care over us, even in difficult times.

THE PROMISES AS A SOCIAL RESPONSIBILITY

"Scripture teaches that the Lord's provision for the needy is to be given through the help and sharing of Christians" (cf. James 2:15-16; 1 John 3:17-18), says Kenneth Van Wyk of the Crystal Cathedral Congregation, Garden Grove, California. "We conclude then that starvation of Christians, or any human being, is not God's plan. It does, however, happen and this is due to the fallenness of the world and the inadequate response of God's people to feed the starving."

He goes on to say, "If we as a country, or more specifically—Chris-

tians, would do what we ought, the world would not see starvation."
That is the essence of one congressional study that reports, "The
world now has the potential to feed ten times the present
population."

Christianity Today concludes, "A mere tithe from the 52 largest US
denominations would yield $17.5 billion annually. Instead, they gave
only $4.4 billion in total church giving (with most of that staying in-
side the church)."

"Two-thirds of the world's nations face recurring suffering for lack
of such basic necessities as food, water, shelter and clothing," according to Ted Engstrom, president of World Vision.

> At World Vision, we acknowledge the existence of suffering and in-
> justice in the world, but focus on our call from God to provide as-
> sistance to the poor and hungry in every way He allows. So we feed
> the hungry, clothe the naked, encourage the downhearted, share
> the good news of the gospel, and work and pray for God's will to be
> accomplished on earth, even as it it in heaven. To sum it up, God
> asks us to minister, even as Christ ministered, to all who are in
> need, and trust in His sovereignty over all things.

This view is capsulized by Gordon Chutter in an article written for
World Vision.[2] "Jesus, by his life, set an unparalleled example. He
identified with deprivation in his life-style, but sought eradication of it
in those to whom he ministered. Of his would-be followers, he required voluntary withdrawal from their self-sufficiency. And the practice of giving—even out of one's own need—was a frequent test of
commitment."

The bottom line of this view, then, is this: Unless we as evangelical
Christians are willing to sacrifice and do our part to lessen the pains
of starvation in the world, we do not have the right to go to God, asking Him to take care of His children. God has ordained Christians to
see to that.

THE PROMISES AS A GUIDING PRINCIPLE

The perspective that most closely aligns itself with an overall view
of Scripture sees these promises of provision as a guiding principle.
Yes, God did provide over and over for the needs of His people, but a

2. Gordon A. Chutter, "Riches and Poverty in the Book of Proverbs," *Together* (Mon-
rovia, Calif.: World Vision International) Issue 3, April-June 1984, p. 31. See also
Ron Sider, *Living More Simply* (Downers Grove, Ill.: InterVarsity, 1980).

quick look at Hebrews 11 will reveal that there were times when God's intervention did *not* occur. Says H. Wayne House,

> The reason I believe it is important to view this question from the principle aspect is mainly due to logic. Let's look at Proverbs 10:3 for example which says "The Lord will not allow the righteous to hunger." Taking this verse to its logical end, one who believes that the righteous will not hunger (we're not talking about starvation here—just hunger) is forced to conclude that the Apostle Paul (2 Cor. 11:27), the beggar Lazarus (Luke 16), Bartimaeus, the blind beggar (Mark 10) and even Christ himself (Matt. 21:18) then did not have enough faith to have their needs met, for all hungered.

Herbert Vander Lugt, senior research editor for the Radio Bible Class adds, "I don't think many Christians starve. Yet the promises about food provision must be taken in the same way as those which speak about deliverance from enemies and long life on the earth. God normally provides these earthly blessings. But not always! Sometimes He allows terrible trials among His own. When He does, however, He pours out another kind of abundance." He goes on to say,

> Whenever the Lord makes promises about earthly blessedness, He fulfills them literally for the vast majority of His children. But He reserves the right to permit some of His children to suffer illness, persecution, even death by execution or starvation. When He permits such experiences, He provides special grace. In the final analysis, every child of God is an "other world" person. We are on our way to our real home—heaven.

John MacArthur, pastor of Grace Community Church, Panorama City, California, concludes:

> God knows the end from the beginning. David acknowledged in Psalm 139 that our days are written down in His book "when as yet there was not one of them." And Paul also wrote "all things work together for good to those who love God" (Romans 8:28). Based on this premise then, we can firmly believe that the Lord knows exactly the amount of time and particular circumstances we need until He is through "conforming us to the image of His Son" down here. God has promised to supply all our needs as His children, but He alone knows the parameters of those needs. We can short circuit that through disobedience (like the case with Ananias and Sapphira, or the Corinthians who were weak and some had died because of

taking Communion in an unworty manner). But, of course, even
that is of no surprise to the Lord!

Putting the Puzzle Together

Writing to Timothy, Paul admonishes, "Be diligent to present yourself approved to God as a workman who does not need to be
ashamed, handling accurately the word of truth" (2 Timothy 2:15).

Dealing with the question of starvation or any other issue in Scripture, we must first rid ourselves of any biases apart from the illumina-
tion given us by the Holy Spirit. Second, we must work diligently in
our quest for truth. And third, we need to handle God's word
accurately.

Can a Christian ever die of starvation? The answer is definitely yes.
There have been accounts of Christians dying from malnutrition in
concentration camps. It has also been documented that a group of
missionaries starved to death on a small island when a storm broke
their tiny ship to pieces on the rocks. The skeletons of those missionaries were found some years later. Notes they wrote were found, and
in them the missionaries gave a day-to-day account of their experience until the last survivor became too weak to write.

So the question emerges, If Christians can die of starvation, why
does God allow it to happen? The answer can be obtained from reading the account of Jesus healing the blind man in John 9. When asked
"Rabbi, who sinned, this man or his parents, that he should be born
blind?" Jesus answered, "It was neither that this man sinned, nor his
parents; but it was in order that the works of God might be displayed
in him. We must work the works of Him who sent Me, as long as it is
day; night is coming, when no man can work" (John 9:2-4).

No one dies by accident. God is sovereign. And any trial, whether it
be hunger or sickness, is outlined in God's plan for eternity. As Christians, then, we are admonished to have the faith to believe that whatever happens to any of us in this life happens in order that the works
of God might be displayed.

That is the faith I saw in the lives of my parents when I was grow-
ing up in Central America. On one occasion, with no food on the table and only flour in the cupboard, I recall my parents sitting us down
around the table thanking God for what He had provided. Just then
there came a knock on the door—and there on the porch sat two
bags of groceries! Reading of God's provision is one thing. Experienc-
ing it, however, has given me an unshakable faith in the God who

works all things for our good and His glory.

The God who created us never forsakes us. And those believers who have been chosen by Him to endure deprivation in any sense can know a deeper peace and fullness through that deprivation than any sort of peace and fullness the world can offer. The person who can accept the hardest things from the hand of God as well as the easiest is the one whose faith is most honoring to the Lord.

1. Four views were presented in this chapter on the issue, Can a Christian ever die of starvation?" After reading those views, can they be dovetailed together in any way, or must they remain distinct? Justify your answer.

2. If certain passages (especially in the Psalms and Proverbs) are intended to be used more as guiding principles than as literal interpretations, how are we to treat other "promises" found in those books? Are they conditional as well? Give illustrations to support your claim.

3. Give an example from your life of God supplying your needs. Also give an example of when you requested God to intervene and He did not. What conclusions have you learned from those experiences?

4. As I stated in the beginning of the chapter, my friend believes spending time on a topic such as this is "an intellectual nonsense game." Do you agree with his assessment? Why or why not?

5. Can you think of any other passages that might help in trying to perceive this problem from God's point of view? Share them with the class.

7

Poverty Brings Riches

But in everything commending ourselves as servants of God,
in much endurance, in afflictions, in hardships, in distresses .
. . as sorrowful yet always rejoicing, as poor yet making many
rich, as having nothing yet possessing all things.

—2 Corinthians 6:4, 10

Not long ago I was at a commissioning service for a young couple
headed off for South America. The pastor used the above passage as
his text to emphasize the point that even though they were sacrificing
materially by going (he is an engineer and had numerous high-paying
offers), in reality they possessed "all things"—and would receive from
God's eternal measuring cup for their faithfulness.

As a matter of fact, I do not know of too many full-time Christian
workers who possess much of this world's wealth. They go through
life not only proclaiming the truths of God's Word but also giving of
their means to help others. Like the Levites in the Old Testament,
those involved in Christian service surrender, in large measure, a
right to a place in this world, the honor of this world, and the wealth
of this world. Indeed, it appears that such a one has literally thrown
his life away. But in reality, through surrendering all that he has and is
to Christ, such a person has everything. That is the ideal for the servant of God.

I left the commissioning service uplifted, thinking, *What commitment and dedication, and what sacrifice this couple has made for
God.* Over the course of the next several days, the Scripture passage

kept coming back to my mind. And the more I contemplated it, the more I became convinced that it is not intended just for missionaries but for every believer. The commission should not be put in moth balls until the next missionary goes out. It ought to be applied to your life and mine on a continual basis.

The apostle Paul in 2 Corinthians 6:1 points out that we are "working together with Him." And every student of the Word can quote verses like Romans 7:6, Romans 12:11, and 2 Corinthians 3:6, which declare us to be servants of God. Still, many of us seem to expect God to be our servant, rather than the reverse. In God's economy, He does not separate "spiritual" ministries from "secular" ones. All of us are to be His workers wherever He sends us—whether it be as a missionary in the jungles of Irian Jaya or as chairman of the board of a Fortune 500 company.

I teach a college course entitled Multi-Cultural Problems. One of the units I cover involves the Christian life-style. I recall one student several years back who took 2 Corinthians 6:10 literally. He firmly believed that to "possess all things" he had to have nothing. Another friend of mine went to the point of refusing to buy a home for that reason. Although I do not denounce those interpretations of Paul's statement, I am convinced that the heart of his message is not an appeal for a poverty-level life for Christians but rather for an appropriate attitude concerning this world's goods.

It was that attitude that Jesus was concerned about in Luke 12. In His parable about the rich man, our Lord said,

> Beware, and be on your guard against every form of greed; for not even when one has an abundance does his life consist of his possessions. . . . And do not seek what you shall eat, and what you shall drink, and do not keep worrying. For all these things the nations of the world eagerly seek; but your Father knows that you need these things. But seek for His kingdom and these things shall be added to you. . . . For where your treasure is, there will your heart be also. (Luke 12:15, 29-31, 34)

Part of being a good master is having the ability and willingness to provide for the needs of the workers. And our Lord is the best master possible. In turn, Scripture teaches that our responsibility as servants is that of stewards or caretakers of the Master's possessions. A steward holds the supreme authority under the master. That is how, as believers, we "possess" all things. Because we are the caretakers of His possessions and heirs of His inheritance, what more could we want? In contrast, as we turn our minds back to the rich man in Luke 12, we see that he rejected the role of the steward by embracing the independent mind-set of this world. He felt that it was in his power to do whatever he wanted to with what he had. He declared that he intended to build larger barns, lay up goods, take ease, eat, drink, and be merry. But God said to the rich man, "You fool! This very night your soul is required of you; and now who will own what you have prepared? So is the man who lays up treasure for himself, and is not rich toward God" (Luke 12:20-21).

CHRISTIAN STEWARDSHIP

May I say, at the risk of sounding judgmental, that the independent attitude that characterized the rich man in Luke 12 is quite similar to that of many Christians I have known. They failed to firmly adopt God's directives in the matter of stewardship.

How we handle money tells much of who and what we are. Sixteen of the thirty-eight parables in the Bible deal with money and possessions. One in ten verses in the gospels also deals with money and possessions. It is interesting to note that there are over five hundred verses in the Bible that talk about faith and approximately the same number on prayer, but there are over two thousand verses on the issue of money.

A good friend of mine who is an economist and accountant told me that 80 percent of the families in America spend over 100 percent of their income. That means there is a lot of borrowing going on. It is also estimated, he said, that 50 percent of all Americans are slaves to debt![1] And the reason many Christians fall into this trap is because they have either not been grounded in the biblical principles of Christian stewardship, or they merely choose to ignore them. The foundation for Christian stewardship, which can be summarized in five points, goes against the prevailing philosophy of our modern society at every turn. Hence, we must be very strong and constantly on guard that we do not fall prey to the "If I want it, somehow I'll get it" philosophy of the world.

---

1. Johnny Williams is a Certified Public Accountant and economist. Currently he is treasurer at LeTourneau College, Longview, Texas. He also teaches in the Business Department of the college.

GOD OWNS EVERYTHING

We as believers are doubly owned, created by God and bought back (redeemed) by His blood. Whereas the world glorifies independence and self-determination, we ought to rejoice in the truth of God's sovereign ownership. Verses that indicate this principle include:

> The earth is the Lord's, and all it contains,
> The world, and those who dwell in it. (Psalm 24:1)

> . . . Remember the Lord your God, for it is He who is giving you power to make wealth. (Deuteronomy 8:18)

> . . . Do you not know that your body is a temple of the Holy Spirit who is in you, whom you have from God, and that you are not your own? For you have been bought with a price: therefore glorify God in your body. (1 Corinthians 6:19-20)

GOD CONTROLS EVERYTHING

It is important to realize that God is in control of this universe, not us. In his praise to God, David says,

> Thine, O Lord, is the greatness and the power and the glory and the victory and the majesty, indeed everything that is in the heavens and the earth; Thine is the dominion, O Lord, and Thou dost exalt Thyself as head over all. Both riches and honor come from Thee, and Thou dost rule over all, and in Thy hand is power and might; and it lies in Thy hand to make great, and to strengthen everyone. (1 Chronicles 29:11-12)

GOD WILL PROVIDE

As faithful stewards, God will provide for our needs (although not necessarily for all our wants). Consequently our attitude toward our needs ought to rest in the security of God's provision for us, as the apostle Paul states: "Be anxious for nothing, but in everything by prayer and supplication with thanksgiving let your requests be made known to God. . . . And my God shall supply all your needs according to His riches in glory in Christ Jesus (Philippians 4:6, 19).

GOD GIVES THAT WE WILL GIVE

God gives to us in order that we may in turn help others. Good stewardship, then, involves service.

> Be hospitable to one another without complaint. As each one has received a special gift, employ it in serving one another, as good stewards of the manifold grace of God. (1 Peter 4:9-10)

> Through love serve one another. . . . So then, while we have opportunity, let us do good to all men, and especially to those who are of the household of the faith. (Galatians 5:13; 6:10)

GOD HOLDS US ACCOUNTABLE

Finally, God holds each of us accountable for what He has entrusted to us. Accountability was the theme Jesus had in mind when He presented the parable of the talents in Matthew 25:14-30. Whether we have been entrusted with much or little, producing to our full capacity with what we have been given is the basis upon which we all will be judged.

THE RESULTS OF STEWARDSHIP

When we base our stewardship values on these principles, true contentment will result. And true contentment is what the world longs for so desperately. The apostle Paul put these principles in their proper perspective.

> Not that I speak from want; for I have learned to be content in whatever circumstances I am. I know how to get along with humble means, and I also know how to live in prosperity; in any and every circumstance I have learned the secret of being filled and going hungry, both of having abundance and suffering need. I can do all things through Him who strengthens me. (Philippians 4:11-13)

> Do you want to be truly rich? You already are if you are happy and good. After all, we didn't bring any money with us when we came into this world, and we can't carry away a single penny when we die. So we should be well satisfied without money if we have enough food and clothing. But people who long to be rich soon be-

gin to do all kinds of wrong things to get money, things that hurt
them and make them evil-minded and finally send them to hell itself. For the love of money is the first step toward all kinds of sin.
Some people have even turned away from God because of their
love for it, and as a result have pierced themselves with many sor-
rows. Oh, Timothy, you are God's man. Run from all these evil
things and work instead at what is right and good, learning to trust
Him and love others, and to be patient and gentle. (1 Timothy 6:6-
11, TLB*)

As we are faithful to God's directives of stewardship, it will become
evident in every area of our daily routine. God expects faithfulness in
our work:

Whatever you do, do your work heartily, as for the Lord rather than
for men. (Colossians 3:23)

in our ethics:

Wherefore it is necessary to be in subjection, not only because of
wrath, but also for conscience' sake. . . . Render to all what is due
them: tax to whom tax is due; custom to whom custom; fear to
whom fear; honor to whom honor. (Romans 13:5, 7)

in our planning and budgeting:

Know well the condition of your flocks, and pay attention to your
herds; for riches are not forever, nor does a crown endure to all
generations. (Proverbs 27:23-24)

in our saving:

There is precious treasure and oil in the dwelling of the wise, but a
foolish man swallows it up. (Proverbs 21:20)

in our sharing and giving:

In everything I showed you that by working hard in this manner
you must help the weak and remember the words of the Lord Jesus,
that He Himself said, "It is more blessed to give than to receive."
(Acts 20:35)

* *The Living Bible.*

and in our attitude:

> He who is faithful in a very little thing is faithful also in much; and he who is unrighteous in a very little thing is unrighteous also in much. (Luke 16:10)

TITHING: A MISAPPROPRIATED DOCTRINE

A chapter on Christian stewardship would not be complete without at least briefly addressing the topic of tithing. The passage most quoted in the pulpit on tithing comes from Malachi.

> Will a man rob God? Yet you are robbing Me! But you say, "How have we robbed Thee?" In tithes and offerings. . . . "Bring the whole tithe into the storehouse, so that there may be food in My house, and test Me now in this," says the Lord of hosts, "if I will not open for you the windows of heaven, and pour out for you a blessing until it overflows." (Malachi 3:8, 10)

Let me say at the outset that the following remarks are in no way intended to demean or depreciate our responsibility before God of giving. What will be the main concern here is the method of giving.

Most churches today teach a fairly easy and traditional approach to Christian giving. Many denominations inculcate what is called "storehouse tithing." Simply put, that view holds that 10 percent of our income must be given to God and that that amount must be given in total to the local church. Any additional gift, they teach, whether it be to a missionary or any worthy cause, is to be considered an "offering" rather than a part of the tithe.

To understand properly any biblical subject or doctrine, we use *hermeneutics*, the process of determining truth. One of the laws of hermeneutics is that Scripture validates itself. Therefore, by looking at all Scriptures pertaining to a subject, we are able to see the eternal truth that is taught. However, many people tend to take one verse or passage out of context and try to build a truth on one it. So if storehouse tithing is a truth of God intended for us to use as doctrine today, then the rest of Scripture, especially the New Testament, will corroborate it. With that in mind, let us look at the Scriptures that deal with our giving to the Lord.

MALACHI 3:7-10

Malachi was written as an appeal to the Jews to keep the law. The tithe was that which they "owed God" under the law. Notice that Malachi uses the word "rob" in verse 8. That is not the kind of word used to denote a gift; rather, it refers to a debt owed by God's people. The people were under obligation, just as we are under obligation to pay taxes today.

A second problem is that the people were told to bring the tithes into the storehouse. That cannot be equated with the local church today. In context, the storehouse was the Temple treasury of Israel. God had structured Israel's government as a theocracy, and the tithe was not a gift; it was more like an income tax. To paraphrase verses 7-10, "The bills are not paid. I have met My end of the contract," God says, "but you Israel have not done your part. Therefore I will withdraw My blessings from you."

We have no Temple today; we have no Temple treasury; we are not under the law; we are not Israel. Thus this passage is not meant to describe a method of giving, but it should be used as an encouragement to obey.

THE MOTIVE FOR CHRISTIAN GIVING

Our motive in giving is not derived from compulsion. It originates from the love and gratitude we have for God because of what He has done for us. As the apostle Paul states, "Let each one do just as he has purposed in his heart; not grudgingly or under compulsion; for God loves a cheerful giver" (2 Corinthians 9:7).

The motive for giving is gratitude; and that motive alone produces a cheerful giver. No one should give because the preacher delivers a sermon on giving; no man should give to get the approval of other men; no one should give merely because it is a special occasion. We ought to give because of the mercies of God, because we love Him and appreciate what He has done for us.

If we give to the Lord cheerfully, joy will result. Paul commends the saints in Macedonia, "that in a great ordeal of affliction their abundance of joy and their deep poverty overflowed in the wealth of their liberality" (2 Corinthians 8:2). Those Christians were joyful, so they gave. Even though they experienced "deep poverty," they willingly gave. And in that way they were rich beyond belief.

Joy and gratitude should be the only motives for Christian giving. Publicizing matching gifts ("if you give so much, I'll give you so much") is an unscriptural method for Christian giving. It is instead the way of the business world. For to whom do we give when we take this attitude? Who gets the glory? Taking the whole idea a little further, let me ask, When we put money into the offering plate, are we giving it to that local church? No, in the deepest sense we are giving it to God.

I believe much of our giving could be classified right along with the accusation Jesus directed toward the Pharisees when He said, "Beware of practicing your righteousness before men to be noticed by them; otherwise you have no reward with your Father who is in heaven" (Matthew 6:1).

THE METHOD OF NEW TESTAMENT GIVING

I would briefly like to bring out seven principles for New Testament giving.

(1) New Testament giving is dedicated giving. In 2 Corinthians 8:5 Paul commends those who "first gave themselves to the Lord."

(2) Giving should be voluntary (2 Corinthians 8:3, 12). You may give 1 percent, 9 percent, 10 percent, 20 percent—10 percent is only one of a hundred possibilities. The key is to ask the Lord what percentage of our income to give. Most of those who hold to the strict literal meaning of the tithe fail to realize that for the Jews approximately 25 percent of their income was considered their tithe. They paid the Levites 10 percent (Leviticus 27:30-33), 10 percent went for sacred ceremonies of praise (Deuteronomy 12:5-6, 11), 3 percent (a tithe of a tithe) went to the strangers, fatherless, and widows (Deuteronomy 14:28-29), to name only some of the amount a Jew needed to give. So if the literal principle of tithing is still for today, we will need to up our giving to over 25 percent.

(3) Giving should be sacrificial (2 Corinthians 8:3; 9:6). There is no way we can outgive God. Paul said the Macedonian church gave "beyond their ability." As we shovel it out, God shovels it in, and His shovel is bigger than ours.

(4) Giving should be proportionate. We need to be constantly aware that everything we own belongs to God. So instead of asking *What shall I give?* we should ask, *What shall I keep?* First Corinthians 16:2 indicates that the amount given should be proportionate to how God has blessed us. What constitutes proportionate giving? Maybe it is equivalent to a week's grocery money, a car payment, or even a house payment—that is between you and God.

(5) Our giving should be "cheerful" (2 Corinthians 8:2; 9:7). The closest word in our English language to this is "hilarious." We should

be excited to give what we have to God's work.

(6) Giving should be done in private. First Corinthians 16:2 admonishes the Christian to "put aside and save." Privately we should seek the Holy Spirit's guidance in distributing the money God has entrusted to us. First Timothy 5, for example, indicates that it is sometimes necessary to give to our family; Acts 6 and Romans 12 state we are to give to needy saints; Galatians 6 tells us to support missionaries; and in the same chapter, as well as in 1 Timothy 5, we see that teachers of God's Word ought to receive our gifts. Giving, then, should be spread out as the Holy Spirit directs us. That means that a local church does not have claim on all our money, but rather it is one of many places God may choose to use our gifts to Him.

(7) Finally, our giving should be systematic. As 1 Corinthians 16:2 states, "On the first day of every week let each one of you put aside and save, as he may prosper, that no collections be made when I come." In the Greek, "putting aside" means to "choose before another thing," or "intend." Thus Christian giving should involve planning and organization.

The responsibility to give is something that every Christian has. We will be judged at the judgment seat of Christ in regard to our stewardship, not only in terms of our finances, but in terms of our life as well. And if we spend our money foolishly, gratifying ourselves without regard for the needs of the gospel, we can expect to lose God's blessing. We will be held accountable. We will not be called into account regarding a 10 percent tithe, but rather we will be called into account regarding our obedience to the Holy Spirit's leading in our life.

As S. Lewis Johnson once said, "Make all you can, but don't can all you make!"[2] We need to make sure before God to give as He desires us to give. I have heard Christians say, "If I am liberal with what I have, I will not have anything left!" To those believers I say, Who gave you what you have? Yes, you worked hard for it . . . but who enabled you to work for that and gave you the mind to think? The answer is God. And God can take it all away tomorrow if He desires.

When we give, God is able to give it all back (see, e.g., the story of Job). And, generally speaking, that is what He will do.

---

2. I credit much of my thinking on the subject of tithing to S. Lewis Johnson (formerly of Dallas Seminary, now guest lecturer at Trinity Evangelical Divinity School). As a youngster, I had the privilege of sitting under his teaching at a church that he pastored in Dallas.

STUDY QUESTIONS

1. It was shown that we are stewards of God's world. How does that affect the way we ought to give?
2. On what basis should we decide how much to spend on a house, what car to buy, and so on?
3. How do you respond to the chapter's critique of storehouse tithing?
4. In order to avoid taxes, legitimate loopholes are used by many people. Consequently their money is tied up, making it difficult for them to give generously to others. How should we respond to that practice?
5. Explain how giving habits closely relate to spiritual maturity.

PART 4

NOBODY KNOWS THE TROUBLE I'VE SEEN

8

Trouble Brings Joy

Consider it all joy, my brethren, when you encounter various
trials, knowing that the testing of your faith produces endurance. . . . Blessed is a man who perseveres under trial; for
once he has been approved, he will receive the crown of life,
which the Lord has promised to those who love Him.

—James 1:2-3, 12

James, do you mean what I think you said? Am I to equate joy with
trials? How can trouble really bring joy? As paradoxical as the admonition appears, however, the fact remains, and God's promise stands
sure. If I choose to live in an attitude and life-style of joy (even when I
encounter trials), some of the benefits I will receive include faith, pa-
tience, strength, wisdom, stability, a perfecting of my character, and a
hope for the future.

But what exactly does James mean when he tells us to rejoice?
What and how do we "consider it all joy?" According to Harold
Fickett,

> James is not telling them to rejoice in the face of the testing exper-
> ience. No one in his right mind rejoices because the doctor tells
> him he has cancer. So what is James trying to say? The word [con-
> sider] should be translated, "think forward." As you live in the pre-
> sent consider the future, think forward to the future. Gloom now,
> but glory in the days to come.[1]

1. Harold L. Fickett, Jr., *James* (Glendale, Calif.: Regal, 1972), pp. 6-7.

Rejoicing in the midst of our trials is also emphasized by the apostle Peter:

> In this you greatly rejoice, even though now for a little while, if necessary, you have been distressed by various trials, that the proof of your faith, being more precious than gold which is perishable, even though tested by fire, may be found to result in praise and glory and honor at the revelation of Jesus Christ. (1 Peter 1:6-7)

There is a difference between joy and happiness in Scripture. Happiness is tied to earthy circumstances; joy will transcend circumstances, because it is related to something infinitely more stable and secure. Joy comes because of and through (1) a believer's *faith* in God—He is sovereign and in control of the events of this world; (2) a believer's *hope*, which is founded on God's eternal promises; and (3) a believer's *love* for God and others. Joy, then, according to Stuart Briscoe, "is one of the most powerful Christian distinctives that needs to be modeled before a happiness crazed society."[2]

Commenting further on this passage in 1 Peter, J. Vernon McGee has this encouraging word to say:

> We need to remember that trials are only temporary (2 Corinthians 4:17, 18). The things at our fingertips are not really of value. They are simply passing things when measured in the perspective of eternity. All these things are destructible. They are corruptible, and they can be defiled. The things of this world do fade away. The things we cannot see are the eternal things. They are of real value.[3]

Kenneth Wuest adds, "Surely this present time is a little while compared to eternity. And then a loving God sees to it that even in the midst of the shadows and heartaches, His children have their days of sunshine in this life."[4]

However, I have discovered that many of the Christians I have counseled seem to approach life in a negative way. They tend to view *all* of life's events as trials, instead of realizing that trials are intended to be specific times and events that God uses to mature His children.

The words in 1 Peter 1:6, "even though now for a little while, if necessary," state the hypothetical rather than the affirmative. That is,

---

2. Stewart Briscoe, *When the Going Gets Tough* (Ventura, Calif.: Regal, 1984), p. 27.
3. J. Vernon McGee, *I Peter* (Pasadena: Thru the Bible, 1983), p. 28.
4. Kenneth S. Wuest, *Wuest's Word Studies from the Greek New Testament,* vol. 2 (Grand Rapids: Eerdmans, 1966), p. 24

they do not say there is *always* a need for the dark days testing and difficulty. In some lives, there seems to be more need of trials than in others. To those servants of God whom He proposes to use in larger, greater ways, many trials are allowed to come, for "we must be ground between the millstones of suffering before we can become bread for the multitude."[5]

Both James and Peter make it quite clear that the Christian life is not a bed of ease. It is instead a rigorous time of training. And although the specific trials we face will not necessarily be ongoing, we can conclude with William Barclay that

> The Christian must expect to be jostled by trials on the Christian way. All kinds of experiences will come to us. There will be the test of sorrows and the disappointments which seek to take away our faith. There will be the test of the seductions which seek to lure us from the right way. There will be the test of dangers, the sacrifices, the unpopularity which the Christian way must so often involve. But they are not meant to make us fall; they are meant to make us soar. They are not meant to defeat us; they are meant to be defeated. They are not meant to make us weaker; they are meant to make us stronger. Therefore we should not bemoan them; we should rejoice in them.[6]

I saw the reality of this truth while counseling the parents of Jennifer, a fifteen-year-old girl who had become pregnant. I remember when Ann, Jennifer's mother, first came to my office. The stress from the situation was almost too much for her to bear. Ann could not think straight, she was depressed, and she carried an extreme amount of guilt. She asked questions like, "Where did I go wrong?" and "What could we have done differently? I feel like God is so distant. Where is He when I need Him?"

However, over a period of time that included weekly counseling sessions, I could see that God was using the trial to bring the family together and to change some priorities that had developed over the years. By no means has the ordeal been easy. There has been the gossip. The family has felt a degree of rejection even by their local church, along with the deep pain involved in seeing their daughter bear a child she cannot keep. And even though Satan desired to use

5. Ibid., p. 25.
6. William Barclay, *The Letters of James and Peter* (Philadelphia: Westminister, 1976), pp. 42-43.

the situation as a means to destroy that Christian family, they were able to rejoice in the difficult time and emerge victors.

WHERE IS GOD WHEN I NEED HIM?

"Where is God when I need Him?" "Why is it that when I am going through a difficulty I feel so lonely?" Ann had initially asked both those questions. But the questions are not unique to her: most believers have at least silently asked the same questions at one time or another.

It has been said that the true test of our character is revealed in the midst of a crisis. What comes into our mind about God at such a time is probably the most important thing that can be said about us.

From my years of counseling I have found that it is easy to acknowledge God and rejoice when all is going well. It is another thing, however, to acknowledge Him and rejoice when our lives are interrupted by a detour. You see, in a crisis our mind may not respond if it is in a vise. Consequently it is difficult to see God working, because the pressure of the moment weighs us down. Also, in a crisis our external mask is stripped away and the true person is revealed. We can wear the super-spiritual mask when all is going well. It is quite another thing to practice what we preach when going through a trial. That is when the validity and depth of our Christianity is tested. And that is why many Christians have such difficulty during the storms of life—because they have not transferred a head-knowledge about God into a heart-knowledge of trust and love.

As we have pointed out in James and 1 Peter, we are told what to expect as Christians. Understanding and accepting those truths provides us with the road map we need to withstand the detours and stresses of life. And if we learn how to respond to the trials of life when things are going well, that foundation, which is based on the truths and principles of God's Word, will carry us through difficult times.

As was mentioned earlier, when we do not perceive God to be nearby during the hard times, the reason may be a lack of spiritual training, maturity, and insight; or the reason may be due to the "tunnel vision" we get when weighted down with a problem.

There is yet another reason. For purposes of our spiritual growth, or for reasons we may not know or understand until we get to heaven, there may be times when each of us will not perceive God as near. At that point we as Christians have the tendency to go to God and ask the highly emotional question, *Why? Lord, I love You and have obeyed You; I have been through Your "spiritual boot camp." I'm a seasoned soldier of Yours, yet You seem to let me down.* Have you ever talked to God this way? I have.

The psalmist was not expressing a feeling unique to him when he cried out to God:

> Why dost Thou stand afar off, O Lord?
> Why dost Thou hide Thyself in times of trouble?
> How long, O Lord? Wilt Thou forget me forever?
> How long wilt Thou hide Thy face from me?
>
> My God, my God, why hast Thou forsaken me?
> Far from my deliverance are the words of my groaning.
> O my God, I cry by day, but Thou dost not answer;
> And by night, but I have no rest.
> Yet Thou art holy.
>
> (Psalm 10:1; 13:1; 22:1-3)

David, the "man after God's own heart," also felt an estrangement from his Creator. Even though he questioned God on the matter, he nevertheless based his life on a solid commitment to Him, rather than relying on his emotions.

Many believers today have trouble identifying with David's last statement because of what psychologists have termed an "entitlement mind-set," a by-product of the humanistic mind-set. The term is defined as "a right to do or have something; or, to give a legal right or claim to something."[7] Instead of simply acknowledging that the God who is holy and all-wise has no need to explain His actions, we fight to understand. We argue when we do not get answers, and we become bitter when things do not go our way. Yet Scripture often tells us that we cannot demand that God explain why He does what He does or allows what He allows (e.g., Job 38-40; Romans 9; 11:33-36). We are promised, however, that "it is God who is at work in you, both to will and to work for His good pleasure" (Philippians 2:13).

The fact that God is sovereign and does not feel the need to explain Himself is a hard pill to swallow for those of us who like to know the reasons for everything. Yet it is extremely important to remember that the attitude we take when we feel that God stands far off be-

---

7. *The American Heritage Dictionary of the English Language* (Boston: American Heritage and Houghton Mifflin, 1975).

comes the key ingredient in achieving victory in trial.

Let us briefly look at three individuals in Scripture who experienced this feeling and see how they responded. For the sake of therapy, it would be a good idea to put ourselves in their shoes and attempt to feel what they must have felt going through their trials.

JOSEPH

The first biblical character I would like to draw our attention to is Joseph. If anybody could argue that God had put him on a detour and then forgot where He put him, it was Joseph. He was hated by his brothers; he was mocked and teased. And if that was not enough, he was sold—a loss of his identity. Most of us would need years of therapy to overcome such treatment. In the new land of Egypt he probably experienced culture shock and had to learn of new ways. He rose to the challenges and proved himself, only to fall again after being falsely accused, thrown into prison, and forgotten.

After what must have seemed an interminable wait, there came that golden opportunity for freedom. Joseph was called upon to interpret the dreams of the butler and and baker. After successfully doing that, Joseph entreated the butler, "Only keep me in mind when it goes well with you, and please do me a kindness by mentioning me to Pharaoh, and get me out of this house (Genesis 40:14). But what happened? "Yet the chief cupbearer did not remember Joseph, but forgot him" (40:23).

Can you not hear Joseph saying, "Now, God, this detour has gone on long enough. I am now refined. I have paid the price. I have been faithful to You. Why then do You treat me like this? Why is there no end to this trial?"

The answer did not come for a while, but eventually the "why" was revealed. He had been held in exactly the right place until exactly the right time for the exact purposes of God. As Joseph told his brothers,

> And God sent me before you to preserve for you a remnant in the
> earth, and to keep you alive by a great deliverance. Now, therefore,
> it was not you who sent me here, but God; and He has made me a
> father to Pharaoh and lord of all his household and ruler over all the
> land of Egypt. (45:6-8)

And later on, he again commented, "Do not be afraid, for am I in God's place? And as for you, you meant evil against me, but God meant it for good in order to bring about this present result, to preserve many people alive" (50:19-20).

LAZARUS'S RELATIVES

The second passage comes from John 11 and deals with the death of Jesus' good friend Lazarus. Lazarus's sisters openly voiced their belief that Jesus had taken an unnecessary detour and could have arrived in time if He had only wanted to. In the account of this story, we vividly see the human reaction to trial.

> Martha therefore said to Jesus, "Lord, if You had been here, my brother would not have died.". . . Therefore, when Mary came where Jesus was, she saw Him, and fell at His feet, saying to Him, "Lord, if You had been here, my brother would not have died.". . . But some of them [the Jews] said, "Could not this man, who opened the eyes of him who was blind, have kept this man also from dying?" (John 11:21, 32, 37)

To Mary, Martha, and the Jews near to the family Christ's power was in healing, not in resurrecting someone from the dead. When Christ did appear on the scene, the only thing they could ask or think was, "Lord why did You wait to come?"

To His disciples Jesus revealed why He had not intervened in the trial of his good friends: "This sickness is not unto death, but for the glory of God, that the Son of God may be glorified by it. . . . Lazarus is dead, and I am glad for your sakes that I was not there, so that you may believe (John 11:4, 14-15).

When we feel that God is far off, we need to remember that in reality He is very near and that He cares for us as a father cares for his child. How obviously that is portrayed in this passage:

> Now Jesus loved Martha, and her sister, and Lazarus. . . . When Jesus therefore saw her weeping, and the Jews who came with her, also weeping, He was deeply moved in spirit, and was troubled, and said, "Where have you laid him?" They said to Him, "Lord, come and see." Jesus wept. (John 11:5, 33-36)

"Jesus wept." The shortest verse in the whole Bible, but what a message for us when we are going through the trials of life. God is not up in heaven looking for ways to make our lives difficult. There are times, however, when for our good and His glory our Savior says

"Wait." And though we don't understand the reason for our trial, we must remember that He does indeed love us and is concerned for us, even when we do not see an answer or feel His closeness.

THE MAN BORN LAME

In Acts 3 we read of a lame man who had been carried to the Temple every day "in order to beg alms of those who were entering the temple" (v. 2). According to 4:22, that had gone on for over forty years. Putting the puzzle together from a statement made by Jesus in Matthew 26:55 (Jesus Himself was in the Temple every day), we can deduce that Jesus was quite aware of this beggar, although He never chose to heal him.

Putting ourselves in the shoes of the lame man, we can see and feel life passing us by much as he must have felt. As a child he could not play with his friends. As a young man he could not get married and have a family of his own. He may even have seen Jesus around the Temple and observed Him healing others. But there he was, still lame.

Why did God pass him by? Was it meanness? No. According to Acts 4:4, Jesus did not heal him so that more than five thousand people could become Christians. His forty years of waiting brought great glory to God.

When God allows us to be tried, when He puts us on a detour or gives us a handicap, do we argue with Him, complain, and become bitter? Or do we acknowledge His sovereignty and put our irrevocable trust in Him because He is God? That is the essence of faith, for faith is not belief without proof; it is trust without reservation.

WRAP-UP

Several years ago I taught at Toccoa Falls College in Georgia. That college suffered the trial of a flood that killed many of my friends and colleagues. A year after the flood, my friend David Eby, who survived the ordeal, made two statements that sum up this discussion on trials.

> I have learned two things from this flood. First, God does not reveal His love to us through circumstances alone . . . He reveals His love by His finished work at Calvary! And second, when we ask the "Why" question in bad times, we must also ask the "Why" question in good times. God doesn't owe us the good life![8]

8. David Eby, currently dean of men at Toccoa Falls College, was miraculously saved during the flood that killed many people. In fact, his house was swept away; but he and his family were saved, even though families downstream all perished.

Christians, I have been told, are like tea bags. Our real strength does not emerge until we are put in hot water. When an ivy league college came to study the stress level at Toccoa several months later, the overall anxiety level was much less than what they expected. The research team could only conclude that it was due to the strong faith in God exhibited by the survivors of the flood—faith that saw beyond the pain to the joy of the eternal reunion and glory to follow.

STUDY QUESTIONS

1. Read Psalm 57, and describe David's response of praise and joy in the midst of trial.
2. Stuart Briscoe described America as a "happiness crazed society." Give some illustrations.
3. Tell of an instance in which you experienced joy when going through a trial and an instance in which you did not experience joy. What made the difference?
4. Why would a humanist dislike the following statement: "Our attempt to comprehend God is like a child scooping a hole in the sand and trying to pour the ocean into it with a seashell"? (Saint Augustine)
5. From a study of James 1 and 1 Peter 1, what kinds of trials beset many of the early Christians? What is the difference between trials and testings?

9
Weakness Brings Strength

And because of the surpassing greatness of the revelations,
for this reason, to keep me from exalting myself, there was
given me a thorn in the flesh, a messenger of Satan to buffet
me—to keep me from exalting myself! Concerning this I entreated the Lord three times that it might depart from me.
And He has said to me, "My grace is sufficient for you, for
power is perfected in weakness." Most gladly, therefore, I
will rather boast about my weaknesses, that the power of
Christ may dwell in me. Therefore I am well content with
weaknesses, with insults, with distresses, with persecutions,
with difficulties, for Christ's sake; for when I am weak, then
am I strong.

—2 Corinthians 12:7-10

Besides taxes and death, suffering can be classified as a surety of
life. Even so, we tend to view suffering and sickness as weakness—ob-
stacles to personal identity or previously defined goals. As a result,
America spends more on medicine and visits to the physician than
any other country in the world. Television ads imply that pain should
not be tolerated. The headache that hinders us from having a good
time at a party demands immediate relief. Obviously, we should not
go about seeking pain or suffering. But it is equally wrong to regard it
as the ultimate foe—as most of us do.

That view of pain, suffering, and sickness is derived in part from the
current humanistic philosophy that deifies man and humanizes God.

When man assumes the role of God, his view of himself is changed. He and his desires become the ultimate good, and everything that causes pain and suffering to him becomes evil. Health and prosperity become the essence of what is good. Most Americans—even Christians—either openly or passively accept that mind-set, agreeing that strength is an absence of any weakness. However, Scripture teaches us that strength is derived from weakness. And instead of suffering and sickness being a barrier to success, God, the all-wise and loving Potter, uses exactly that to mold and shape us into the mature believers He desires us to be—believers who are not only useful to the Master but are strong in the true joy and inner resources of the Spirit. In fact, as Christians we are called to suffer. The apostle Peter states,

> For you have been called for this purpose, since Christ also suffered for you, leaving you an example for you to follow in His steps. . . . Therefore, let those also who suffer according to the will of God entrust their souls to a faithful Creator in doing what is right. (1 Peter 2:21; 4:19)

This call to suffering is a paradox for the secularist, who runs from suffering at all costs. It also is perplexing for the fatalist, who is trained to simply resign himself to whatever happens. Fatalism is defined as "the doctrine that all events are predetermined by fate (unfavorable doom, ruin, or destiny) and therefore unalterable by man."[1] Many peoples of the third world carry that perspective of life.

Contrary to those two opinions, there can be real benefit in suffering when it is biblically understood. And when right attitude becomes right living, undeniable and obvious Christlikeness results. That is one of the strongest testimonies we can ever bear before an unbelieving or carnal world, because it is a reflection of our Lord's own suffering and death. It is a most memorable example of what it means to die to self.

For the Christian whose attitude towards suffering is in tune with the biblical directives on the subject, there will come the point when pain begins to build the inner person up, rather than destroying him. Joni Eareckson's story is a beautiful example.[2] After her paralysis there was a time of bitterness, hostility, and anger. It took three years to finally come to the place of adjustment and acceptance, resting in God's

---

1. *The American Heritage Dictionary of the English Language* (Boston: American Heritage, 1975).
2. Joni Eareckson with Joe Musser, *Joni* (Grand Rapids: Zondervan, 1976).

promise, "I came that they might have life, and might have it abundantly" (John 10:10).

The mystery of suffering is indeed a paradox. Pain jostles with triumph and rubs elbows with despair. And yet people like Joni show us that Christians in the worst prison of suffering can still hear God and believe Christ's words, "I have overcome the world!" (John 16:33).

WHY THE EMPHASIS ON OUR WEAKNESSES?

Why does God place an emphasis on weakness rather than strength? There seem to be five basic reasons:

First, it reveals our dependence on God. The psalmist declared, "How blessed is the man whose strength is in Thee; in whose heart are the highways to Zion!" (Psalm 84:5). As creatures of His handiwork, we are not the masters of our own destinies and we cannot live this life on our own strength. Trial and suffering bring that realization home to us in a most graphic way.

Second, God uses weakness to teach us that the earthly achievements accomplished through human strength will eventually erode and become useless. Jesus emphasizes this point when He says,

> Do not lay up for yourselves treasures upon earth, where moth and rust destroy, and where thieves break in and steal. But lay up for yourselves treasures in heaven, where neither moth nor rust destroys, and where thieves do not break in or steal; for where your treasure is, there will your heart be also. (Matthew 6:19-21)

Third, Scripture places an emphasis on weakness because it is simply realistic. The apostle Paul says that a person would be a fool to think otherwise (2 Corinthians 12:6). Whether we accept it or not, our universal weakness as human beings stems from the fact that we cannot proclaim in confidence what our behavior will be or whether we will be able to carry out the plans we have made for today, much less tomorrow. James rebukes the Jewish Christians who have forgotten this truth.

> Come now, you who say, "Today or tomorrow, we shall go to such and such a city, and spend a year there and engage in business and make a profit." Yet you do not know what your life will be like tomorrow. You are just a vapor that appears for a little while and then vanishes away. Instead, you ought to say, "If the Lord wills, we shall

live and also do this or that." But as it is, you boast in your arro-
gance; all such boasting is evil. (James 4:13-16)

Fourth, our weaknesses enable us to give God the credit for any accomplishments. During my high school days I never took a college
preparation course. I was told never to attend college because I probably would not make the grade. Yet God allowed me not only to fin-
ish college but to complete four years of graduate school as well.
There is no way that I can claim credit for what God has accomplished in my life, for He has taken a weakness of mine and has turned
it into a strength. That was also the conclusion of Paul (2 Corinthians
12:7).

It is also important that we realize that when God is in the process
of turning our weaknesses into strengths, He does not give up on us
when we fail. When God chose Moses for the part he was to play in
the Exodus, his obvious weakness was in leadership potential. And after reminding God of all his imperfections—five objections that included such statements as *I'm inferior; I don't have any power; I
don't have any credentials; I can't speak;* and *I'm really scared* (Exodus 3-4), Moses finally realized that all God wanted was an empty ves-
sel willing to be used. He would do the rest.

The fifth reason God emphasizes suffering and weakness instead of
strength and prosperity is that through the former, the Body of Christ
becomes more solidified. We read in the book of Acts (5:40-42) that
the church grew, not as a result of peaceful times, but because of the
need to be interdependent during times of adversity and extreme
persecution.

Paul describes this interdependence:

> The members of the body which seem to be weaker are necessary;
> and those members of the body, which we deem less honorable, on
> these we bestow more abundant honor, and our unseemly
> members come to have more abundant seemliness, whereas our
> seemly members have no need of it. But God has so composed the
> body, giving more abundant honor to that member which lacked,
> that there should be no division in the body, but that the members
> should have the same care for one another. And if one member
> suffers, all the members suffer with it; if one member is honored, all
> the members rejoice with it. (1 Corinthians 12:22-26)

Paul's point is clear. Christ chose to give us weaknesses in order
that the Body of Christ as a whole would benefit. And, in order to

keep the Body from malfunctioning, each member needs not only to contribute but also to receive from the Body when in need.

THE MEANING OF SUFFERING

Because believers are called to suffer, it is important to differentiate the various kinds of pain we can experience. Some kinds of pain and suffering are not part of God's call.

To begin with, a definition of pain is in order. "Pain" comes from the Greek word *ponos,* which means "penalty," for the Greeks looked on pain as a curse. Pain is the consequence of a disease or injury. Pain can be mental (taking an exam), verbal (a result of scolding or taunting), ideological (as when life-style or dogma separates father and son), or compassionate (empathy when a loved one is hurting), as well as physical. Pain is universal, but the degree of tolerance each person exhibits toward pain in each of its forms is directly related to the mental and spiritual attitude of the sufferer.

PAIN TELLS US IMPORTANT THINGS

Pain tells our body when something is wrong. Pain is as essential to a normally functioning body as eyesight or good circulation. Without pain we would be in constant danger.[3] It has been reasoned that teaching children to view pain as an enemy has become one of the major causes for drug abuse among teenagers.[4] In one television account it was pointed out that the worst effect from drug abuse is not biological but rather psychological. In their formative years children should be wisely taught how to cope with the pain, anxiety, and pressures of life. Instead, we try to shield our children from such things. We teach them by our own lives as we silently proclaim that through tranquilizers, pain killers, and alcohol we can make the unhappiness and pain of life go away. Our example eloquently encourages our children toward drug abuse.

PAIN MUST HURT

Pain is, generally speaking, the quickest and best way to bring about necessary and positive change. Working on an artificial nerve

---

3. For an excellent book on this subject, read Paul Brand and Philip Yancey, *Fearfully and Wonderfully Made* (Grand Rapids: Zondervan, 1980).
4. "Teenagers and Drug Abuse," a television documentary produced by NBC and shown 10 December 1978.

cell for leprosy patients whose nerve cells had been destroyed, Dr. Paul Brand's team of researchers studied the question of whether a stimulus needed to be painful for the subject to alter his behavior.

> For a long time they used an audible signal coming through a hearing aid, a signal that would hum when the tissues were receiving normal pressures, and buzz loudly when the tissues were actually in danger. But the signal was not unpleasant enough. A patient would tolerate a loud noise . . . even though the signal told him it could be harmful. . . . Brand finally resorted to electric shock to make people let go of something that might hurt them. People had to be forced to remove their hands; being alerted to the danger was insufficient. The stimulus had to be unpleasant, just as pain is unpleasant.[5]

Dr. Brand was unable to change a leprosy patient's behavior by using an audible signal. Even though the patient knew his sensory-impared limb was in danger when the signal buzzed, that buzz, in and of itself, was not enough to deter his action. Only *pain* could keep the patient from further injury. God obviously understood this aspect of human nature, because much is said in Scripture about the necessarily unpleasant characteristics of discipline (see Proverbs 13:24 and Hebrews 12:5-11 for two examples).

PAIN AND PLEASURE

Pain and pleasure are not diametrically opposed to each other. George Wald, a Nobel prize-winner once stated, "When you have no experience of pain, it is rather hard to experience joy."[6] Being part of a college faculty for over fifteen years, I have observed that the students who must work in order to pay for their education in many cases perform better in the classroom than those who have their total educational cost handed to them on a silver platter. The pain and sweat involved in working through school forces the student to be more serious toward his education. And after the pain, there is joy. Most worthwhile accomplishments involve a long struggle, usually associated with pain. Athletes, musicians, and artists will all be quick to acknowledge that training and practice are indeed painful. Christ

---

5. Philip Yancey, *Where Is God When It Hurts?* (Grand Rapids: Zondervan, 1978), p. 28.
6. George Wald was born in 1906. He joined the faculty of Harvard in 1934. Dr. Wald is noted for his work on the chemistry of vision and was the first to discover that a lack of vitamin A is accompanied by eye infections and night blindness.

compared the passion of the cross and the joy of the resurrection to a mother in labor: after the pain and tears and struggle there is abounding joy. Indeed, it seems that struggle is the launching pad for joy.

PAIN AND DISCIPLINE

Pain is needed to bring about self-discipline. It is the price we must pay in order to win the game of life. The apostle Paul, using the athletic events of the day to emphasize this point, stated:

> Do you not know that those who run in a race all run, but only one receives the prize? Run in such a way that you may win. And everyone who competes in the games exercises self-control in all things. They then do it to receive a perishable wreath, but we an imperishable. Therefore I run in such a way, as not without aim; I box in such a way, as not beating the air; but I buffet my body and make it my slave, lest possibly, after I have preached to others, I myself should be disqualified. (1 Corinthians 9:24-27)

A friend of mine is a prosperous businessman in Tennessee. On a recent trip there, I got conned into jogging with him at 5:30 A.M. While we were jogging I asked how he could force himself to jog every morning—especially when the warm bed was so enticing. His reply was, "I must force myself to do something every day that I do not like to do. When I do, my mind reminds me of it when I am working on a hard project or struggling at a task that I would like to abandon, even though I know the end result will be of great benefit." One who has never learned to struggle may be the one who first abandons the battle.

PAIN THAT IS OUR OWN FAULT

Some pain is unnecessary because it is the consequence of our own actions. "Do not be deceived, God is not mocked; for whatever a man sows, this he will also reap" (Galatians 6:7). God used pain as a punishment against Babylon for mistreating His people Israel: "And they will be terrified, pains and anguish will take hold of them; they will writhe like a woman in labor, they will look at one another in astonishment, their faces aflame" (Isaiah 13:8). In the New Testament we are even told that some in a local church were suffering because they did not come to the Lord's table in the proper manner. Suffering and pain may be the only way God can get our attention when we are headed in a direction different from God's desires.

A word of caution, however. We ought not immediately ascribe all pain and suffering to sin. That view can cause much damage.

PAIN AND PRIORITIES

Pain or suffering enables us to rank our values or priorities. Because we live in such a specialized world, it is easy to get so wrapped up in our jobs or our leisure pursuits that our priorities become distorted. A painful event or accident can help change that attitude for life.

PAIN BROUGHT ON BY CULTURE

Pain may be experienced for cultural reasons. Some examples include puberty rights in some primitive cultures; the plucking of the eyebrows or sunbathing in our culture; the ancient oriental custom of binding a baby girl's feet; and the custom of showing sorrow over the death of a loved one by ritual maiming or disfiguration. Every society has some habits and cultural expectations that are painful, and when it comes right down to it, sometimes even shaving can be a painful cultural experience.

STUDY QUESTIONS

1. When we are suffering, our emotional response to the pain many times becomes as hurtful as the pain itself. How would you help one who has been hurting for a long time—when the pain never seems to go away? Is just quoting Scripture in love enough?
2. How has God turned your weakness into a strength? Tell how you matured spiritually as a result.
3. What is modern man's view of pain and weakness? Why?
4. In what ways can weakness, suffering, or pain be beneficial to a believer? To the Body of Christ?
5. When in your own life have you experienced suffering and struggle to be a launching pad for joy?

10

Suffering Is Beneficial

Is anyone among you suffering? Let him pray. Is anyone cheerful? Let him sing praises. Is anyone among you sick? Let him call for the elders of the church, and let them pray over him, anointing him with oil in the name of the Lord; and the prayer offered in faith will restore the one who is sick, and the Lord will raise him up, and if he has committed sins, they will be forgiven him. Therefore, confess your sins to one another, and pray for one another, so that you may be healed. The effective prayer of a righteous man can accomplish much.

—James 5:13-16

To get a fine-tuned picture of God's promise for strength in the midst of weakness, we must spend some time discussing the doctrine of healing. In Christian circles there is probably no area of teaching that is more misunderstood. Just turn on your radio or television on any Sunday morning or evening, and you will be told that anybody can be healed *if* there is enough faith, *if* twenty-five dollars is sent in for a healing handkerchief, *if* hands are placed on the television or radio. One evangelist has mailed a photocopy of his hands to people, instructing them to place the photocopy on the problem area of their body, as he cannot be there in person. And because those photocopied hands have been prayed over, healing can thus become a reality. There was a P.S. on the letter asking for money.

UNDERSTANDING PAUL'S "THORN"

The "thorn in the flesh" Paul mentions in 2 Corinthians 12:7 was indeed a real sickness. *Astheneia*, the word translated "infirmities" in the King James Version and "weakness" in the *New American Standard Bible* (12:5, 9-10), means disease or sickness. Most commentators agree that the "thorn" in Paul's life was some physical ailment that caused him to suffer greatly.

It is important for us to understand why God chose not to heal Paul, although He willingly healed in other instances. To comprehend that, five pieces of the puzzle need to be put together.

First, we need to remember that *any* healing is divinely ordained. That does not mean that we are always miraculously healed. What it does mean is that because we are divinely made and created, natural healing, which is ordained by God, can take place. Is it any less of a miracle that our blood coagulates when we get a cut, than for us to have a heart attack and one month later be on the tennis court as if nothing happened? The answer is no. We do not have the right to make a hierarchy of God's ways of healing.

Second, the request for healing ought not be motivated by personal benefit, but rather for the propagation of God's work. Dr. Alfred Plummer of Oxford University says, "Paul's request for healing in vs. 8 was not for personal reasons (for in reality he wanted to be in heaven), but for the good of the church. And, when God told him his illness would not hinder his ministry, he then gladly accepted it (vs. 10)."[1]

Third, we must conclude that God miraculously extends His mercy of healing to both the just and the unjust, the Christian and the non-Christian. In my file I have newspaper articles of individuals, some not professing to be Christians, who were miraculously healed after bizarre accidents. We are never told that Naaman was a believer. In the New Testament we are told that God spared some from suffering but not others. Although God is sovereign and we believers are His children, that does not give us the right to demand healing of God.

Fourth, we need to unmask the type of sickness we are dealing with. Many illnesses are psychosomatic in nature *(psycho* = mind; *soma* = body). A psychosomatic illness is a real illness that is caused by psychological problems—for example, ulcers, headaches, muscle aches, weakness resulting from stress. It has been proved that after prolonged and uninterrupted depression the body's defenses are bro-

1. Alfred Plummer, *A Critical and Exegetical Commentary on the Second Epistle of St. Paul to the Corinthians* (Edinburgh: T & T Clark, 1966), pp. 354-55.

ken down. Illnesses can then infiltrate the body. When one relaxes and the stress is eliminated, the body's defenses can once again begin to function, and the symptoms of the illness can disappear. That may be the reason for some miraculous cures at healing meetings. According to Philippians 4, psychosomatic illnesses ought not be a part of the Christian life anyway, because we are not to be anxious or uptight no matter what the circumstances. Two footnotes here: (1) God does miraculously heal individuals. But there is no formula for healing, and He cannot be forced to do so. (2) The glory of all healing must be returned to Christ Himself. At many healing meetings it is the Holy Spirit or a human being who is exalted (John 16:13-14).

Last, not all sickness is a result of a particular sin; but without sin there would be no sickness. We must understand that the root of all pain and suffering is sin. There is a cause and effect relationship here. The cause of all sickness is sin, the effect of sin is evil, including sickness. (When there will be an absence of sin, there will also be an absence of sickness—Revelation 21:4.) Along the same line, the ultimate curse of sin is death for both the Christian and non-Christian. So in reality any physical healing on this earth simply is prolonging the inevitable, which is death.

JAMES 5 ON HEALING

Many Christians use the fifth chapter of James as the foundation for their theology on healing. Basically, evangelicals hold to the following three views on this passage.

REAL SICKNESS + REAL OIL (AS A SYMBOL) + PRAYER = HEALING

Several denominations hold the view that healing is an ordinance of the New Testament church, thus taking the passage at face value. If a believer is sick, he is to call the elders of the church, who will anoint him with oil in the name of the Lord. And if his sins are forgiven and he prays in faith believing, that individual will become well.

REAL SICKNESS + REAL OIL (ASSOCIATED WITH MEDICINE) + PRAYER = HEALING IN ACCORDANCE WITH GOD'S WILL

Those who hold this view point to verses like Isaiah 1:6 that speak of bruises, sores, and wounds that have been treated with oil. In that day, they argue, oil was used as a medicine. Pastoral counselor Jay Adams says,

Olive oil was considered medicinal. In fact, in Biblical times oil was used as the universal medicine (Mark 6:13, Luke 10:34). James contemplated no magic when he mentioned the use of oil. . . . As a matter of fact, James did not write about ceremonial anointing at all (different Greek word). The [Greek] word James used, in contrast . . usually means "to rub" or simply "apply" . . . like a trainer who rubbed down athletes in a gymnastic school. What James advocated was the use of consecrated, dedicated medicine. In this passage he urged the treating of sickness by medical means accompanied by prayer. So instead of teaching faith healing apart from the use of medicine, the passage teaches just the opposite.[2]

SICKNESS (NOT NECESSARILY A PHYSICAL ILLNESS) + OIL USED IN A TOTALLY SYMBOLIC SENSE + PRAYER = UPLIFTING

The Greek word translated "sick" in verse 14 also means lack of strength. It can refer to a runner faltering toward the end of a race and wanting to drop out. Harry A. Ironside, in opting for this view, stated, "In this case, James must have been talking about sickness in the sense of lack of strength, because not all physical sickness will be healed. God may want us to have His strength in our weakness as was the case with the Apostle Paul."[3]

This view postulates that the oil used in this passage as well as in other passages ought to be interpreted in a symbolic sense only (Psalm 23:5; Hebrews 1:9). Oil then is a symbol to signify that uplifting or healing of any kind is received from a power apart from ourselves, an external source that comes from God Himself. The prophet Isaiah adds:

> He gives strength to the weary, and to him who lacks might He increases power. Though youths grow weary and tired, and vigorous young men stumble badly, yet those who wait for the Lord will gain new strength; they will mount up with wings like eagles, they will run and not get tired, they will walk and not become weary. (Isaiah 40:29-31)

Dr. Ironside went on to say that if verse 15 always refers to a real sickness, that would contradict Paul's experience in 2 Corinthians,

2. Jay Adams, *The Christian Counselor's Manual* (Philadelphia: Presbyterian & Reformed, 1975), pp. 107-8.
3. H. A. Ironside, *Addresses on the Second Epistle to the Corinthians* (New York: Loizeaux Brothers, 1954), pp. 262-65.

when he asked three times for his "thorn" to be removed from him.[4] The logical conclusion would be that Paul did not have the faith needed to be healed. However, an understanding of the Greek word for "sick" in verse 15, which can be translated "fatigue," helps answer that problem, because God will deliver a believer from fatigue in times of great pressure but doesn't guarantee healing in times of illness.

WHAT ARE WE TO LEARN FROM THIS PASSAGE?

Regardless of which view of James 5 we take, the major point we can obtain from the passage is that we ought not to expect a life void of sickness or suffering. The Greek word for suffering in verse 13 is *paschō,* meaning to endure or experience pain. The hope comes in knowing that God promises to relieve the fatigue that accompanies our suffering as He journeys with us through our daily struggles (Psalm 23). He has chosen that for us rather than eliminating or insulating us from difficulties (James 5:10-11).

Why, then, is James 5 so needed? This passage is needed for two reasons: (1) The body of Christ cannot function at its best unless all are willing to be unified spiritually, mentally, and socially (1 Corinthians 12:25-27), and (2) we need to use our strengths to help those who are weak, and, conversely, let those who may be strong in areas other than our own help us in our weakness.

SUMMATION: HOW PAIN AND SUFFERING MAY BE USED

God has His purpose in allowing us to suffer. A look at nine ways suffering is used in Scripture can help us identify life situations wherein God works through suffering. It can also help us understand and accept suffering when it occurs in our life.

Suffering and pain may be used (1) to illustrate divine truth (John 11); (2) to purify the believer and make him stronger (1 Peter 1:7-8); (3) to develop the "faith-rest" technique (Romans 5:3); (4) to demonstrate the power of God and His sovereignty (2 Corinthians 11:24-33; Romans 8:38-39; chapter 9); (5) to allow the Christian to be identified with Christ and reign with Him (Romans 8:17; 2 Timothy 2:12; Philippians 2:29); (6) to help others who suffer (2 Corinthians 1:3-6); (7) to enable us to witness for Christ (2 Timothy 2:8-9; Jeremiah 15:16); (8) to correct God's children through divine discipline (He-

4. Ibid.

brews 5:8; 12:6; 1 Corinthians 11:31-32); (9) so that effective empathy can be realized and practiced in the Body (1 Corinthians 12:16; Romans 12:15—"Weep with those weep" implies a transference of pain from one believer to the other).

COPING WITH PAIN ON A DAILY BASIS

It is one thing to tell others how to deal with pain and suffering from a biblical standpoint. It is quite another thing to cope with pain when we are constantly bombarded with chronic problems or illness. There are several suggestions that I would like to present that might help when that does occur.

First, we must accept that mental suffering or physical pain are used to warn us of a problem, and we should treat them as such.

Second, our attitude toward a particular pain is one of the chief factors in how it affects us. Prolonged attention to pain tends to make it worse. In some experiments measuring pain thresholds, scientists found that the ability to withstand or ignore pain went up 19-45 percent just by diverting a person's attention.[5] Thinking about and dwelling on our pain can intensify the pain we experience. Consequently, we need to find useful diversions so that our minds do not becomes obsessed with the suffering at hand. Hence Philippians 4:8, which admonishes us to think of "whatever is of good repute."

Third, we do not have to respond to pain and suffering from a helpless point of view. Fear and helplessness can push a painful experience into the realm of the unbearable. But as Paul states in 2 Timothy 1:7, "God has not given us a spirit of timidity, but of power and love and discipline."

Dr. Curt Richter of Johns Hopkins University found that resigned helplessness in the face of pain and suffering can actually cause a patient to stay sick.[6] Suffering can become a trap for self pity, wounded pride, martyr feelings, and a negative self-image. A healthy, positive attitude, on the other hand, contributes to the healing process.

Fourth, we need to realize that God can use pain to help the believer want to be with Him in heaven. When Dr. J. Robertson McQuilkin, president of Columbia Bible College, was asked by an elderly lady, "Why does God allow us to get old and weak?" he replied:

---

5. Philip Yancey, *Where Is God When It Hurts?* (Grand Rapids: Zondervan, 1978), p. 143.
6. Ibid., pp. 141-42.

I think God has planned the strength and beauty of youth to be physical. But the strength and beauty of age is spiritual. We gradually lose the strength and beauty that is temporary so we'll be sure to concentrate on the strength and beauty that is forever. And so we'll be eager to leave the temporary, deteriorating part of us and be truly homesick for our eternal home. If we stayed young and beautiful, we might never want to leave!"[7]

THE FINAL GOAL OF SUFFERING

A final reason for suffering can be found in Romans 8:28: "And we know that God causes all things to work together for good to those who love God, to those who are called according to His purpose." "All things"—things that include pain and suffering—"work together for good"—like a puzzle. Even though we may not be able to see the benefits to be gained from the suffering, from God's vantage point the puzzle fits together. And it may not be until eternity that the reasons for the pain and suffering are revealed.

There are two qualifications presented in this verse that must be met before we can understand what God is teaching us through pain and suffering. First, we must love God. Without that, the interpretation of suffering will be altered and distorted. Second, suffering is "according to His purpose." God has a purpose in everything He does, regardless of whether we can see it or not. (Romans 11:33 states that God's ways are "unsearchable" and "unfathomable.") A realization that God has a purpose in our suffering, then, helps us to develop a strong faith and trust in God, so that we can depend on Him no matter what He allows to transpire.

The follower of the Lord may experience illnesses and pain just as the nonbeliever does, but there should be a difference. The Christian can emerge more mature, a better person because of what Jesus continues to do in his life through the Holy Spirit. He is better off for having gone through the suffering.

7. Ibid., p. 155.

STUDY QUESTIONS

1. Can we ever be sure that God wants our particular illness to be healed? How do we counsel a Christian who believes God will heal him because he asks in faith?
2. What specific guidelines should be used when praying for a Christian who is ill?
3. What view of James 5 seems the most feasible? Why?
4. Nine ways God uses pain were presented in this chapter. Choose one from the list, and tell how God has used that particular way in your own life.

PART 5

A MATTER OF LIFE AND DEATH

11

To Live Is to Die

And Jesus answered them saying, "The hour has come for the
Son of Man to be glorified. Truly, truly, I say to you, unless a
grain of wheat falls into the earth and dies, it remains by itself
alone; but if it dies, it bears much fruit. He who loves his life
loses it; and he who hates his life in this world shall keep it to
life eternal."

—John 12:23-25

To live is to die? I have to hate my life to keep it? This is perhaps
the one paradox that even Christians stumble over. And, of course,
"enlightened" modern man has no time for such gibberish; he knows
that self worth, self-esteem, and self-fulfillment are absolutely necessary for a good, happy life. In fact, my graduate psychology courses
taught exactly the opposite of Jesus' remarks here. Yet for the believer who is enlightened by the Holy Spirit, this analogy of the need to
die in order to produce fruit "is as universal as harvest and as inexora-
ble as centrifugal force. Applied in a spiritual realm, Jesus impressed
upon His disciples as *essential to their success* this fundamental truth
which He must demonstrate with His own death."[1]

To grasp the essence of this passage, however, it is important to get
a picture of the setting. We see from verse 17 that Lazarus had just
been raised from the dead. The next two verses then focus on wor-

1. Merrill C. Tenney, *John: The Gospel of Belief* (Grand Rapids: Eerdmans, 1960), p.
188.

ried Pharisees, who were afraid the masses might follow Jesus as a result of that miracle.

With that as a backdrop, the audience to whom Jesus addresses His paradoxical statement is found in verse 20. From this verse we can conclude that Jesus was talking to both His disciples and some Greeks. The Greeks had asked to see Jesus, presumably wondering what Christ could do for them (that fact is important to the interpretation of the paradox). We are not told the specific questions that were asked, only the answers given by Jesus. According to Merrill C. Tenney, "The introduction of the Greeks was not incidental, for the discourse of Jesus prompted by their petition was important. It was a declaration of His purpose in coming to earth and of the resolution to fulfill that purpose."[2]

Actually there are two interpretations for verses 23-24. Both are acceptable, but I believe one is more accurate in light of the context.

THE MORE POPULAR EXPLANATION

(1) "The hour has come for the Son of Man to be glorified." This indicates Christ's approaching death. (2) "A grain of wheat" refers to the person of Jesus Christ. (3) "Falls into the earth and dies" speaks of Christ's actual death at Calvary. (4) "It remains by itself alone" means that if Jesus had not died, man would not have had the opportunity for salvation. (5) "But if it dies, it bears much fruit." Because of Calvary, we now have the opportunity to be saved—thus the fruit of His work is salvation for the lost.

THE MORE CONTEXTUAL INTERPRETATION

This explanation is derived when it is taken into consideration that Jesus was answering questions that the Greeks had raised. This second view is, I believe, the passage's primary meaning, with the first explanation as more of a secondary meaning.[3]

(1) "The hour has come" does indeed speak of the impending death of Christ. "For the Son of Man to be glorified" indicates that the time has arrived for the Son of Man (Christ) to be glorified by receiving the worshipful homage of the Gentiles. That was a revolutionary concept, connecting with verse 32, which points out, "And I [Christ],

---

2. Ibid., p. 186.
3. Arthur W. Pink, *Exposition of the Gospel of John*, vol. 2 (Grand Rapids: Zondervan, 1963), pp. 267-70.

if I be lifted up from the earth, will draw all men to Myself." Thus His death would not only be for Jews, but for the Gentiles as well—a specific answer to a question raised by the Greeks.

(2) "A grain of wheat," then, actually refers to the Gentiles, not Jesus.

(3) "Falls into the earth." The Greek word here translated "fall" means "alight or dismount." The new idea Jesus is trying to convey to the Greeks is that they are now held by an external force—which is Satan's control—and in order for them to obtain access to God they must be "dismounted" or "released" from his dominion and power. And the Greeks could be released by accepting the work Jesus was about to do on the cross (Ephesians 2:13).

(4) "And dies, it remains by itself alone." "Die," in the Greek, denotes separation, or a force that causes a reversed action or attitude. That indicates that the Gentiles were encased like a peanut in its shell, unable to break free to obtain the truth, and so for the Gentiles to know God, the shell of the seed had to die, or be broken.

(5) "But if it dies, it bears much fruit." Finally, if there is a breaking free from the control of the god of this world (Satan), *then* much fruit will result. The fruit refers to a future state of eternal life with Christ, a hope that is guaranteed because of the sealing work of the Holy Spirit who preserves all believers until the day of redemption (Ephesians 4:30).

Let's put all the pieces together and paraphrase these two verses. Christ would die for the Gentiles who had previously no hope. But now the Gentiles' shell would be broken (representing Satan's control) through Christ's death. As a result Gentiles can now have hope of eternal life with Him.

THE PARADOX OF THE PASSAGE

The paradox can be found in the next verse: "He who loves his life loses it; and he who hates his life in this world shall keep it to life eternal."

In that verse lies the application of Christ's answer. He had told the Greeks that the shell of Satan's power and control was about to be broken. From now on the Gentiles would have choices—a choice of masters and a choice of priorities. But only someone willing to be enlightened by the Holy Spirit could make the right choices. The choices that seem the right and logical and natural are indeed wrong.

Whether Christ is number one, totally and unquestionably, becomes the pivotal point upon which the direction of our life rests. The major areas affected by that direction will be our priorities and what we think about ourselves.

PRIORITIES

He who loves father or mother more than Me is not worthy of Me; and he who loves son or daughter more than Me is not worthy of Me. And he who does not take his cross and follow after Me is not worthy of Me. He who has found his life shall lose it, and he who has lost his life for My sake shall find it. (Matthew 10:37-39)

Stuart Briscoe in his book *When the Going Gets Tough* says:

The Lord Jesus told His disciples during their training, "Anyone who dares not take up his cross and follow Me is not worthy of Me." Modern-day disciples sometimes complain about their arthritis and bravely say, "I suppose it is my cross." Others regard a difficult marriage in the same way and say, "I suppose we all have our cross to bear." We should never confuse arthritis and husbands with crosses. To take up the cross is not to put up with the inevitable and put on a brave face. Jesus Christ took up His cross intelligently, willingly and joyfully because He knew it was the Father's will. To take up the cross is to accept the will of God in the same manner as Christ did, fully recognizing that it will involve some degree of pain and discomfort as it did for Him.[4]

The cross is the divine divider that separates total commitment from easy believism. When Christ becomes number one, our priorities will reflect a total yielding to His desires, His wishes, and His commands. Even the most noble of loves (mother, father, son, daughter) must take a back seat to our love and devotion and obedience to Him. As we apply Matthew 10:37-39 to the whole of our lives, we realize that even the very best things can become bad if they keep us from responding to Christ as we should with our time, our talents, our financial resources, and so on.

As we delve further into John 12:23-25 and Matthew 10:37-39, we come to see that Christ is referring to two distinct lives, the life of the flesh and the life of the Spirit. With that in mind, Matthew 10:39 could

4. D. Stuart Briscoe, *When the Going Gets Tough* (Ventura, Calif.: Regal, 1984), p. 170.

read, "He who finds his lower (earthly) life will lose his higher (eternal or spiritual) life."

Both the higher and lower life have been identified with the self, yet Christ taught that the higher self becomes the true nature of a believer. Just as the prodigal son "came to himself" and returned home to God, so each of us must decide between the two roads available in life. Each of us is confronted with a choice between flesh or spirit, earth or heaven. No one can choose both. To choose the one is to lose the other. "To find by losing is the principle rightly applied; for this is the mortal surrendering to the immortal. To lose by finding is the principle wrongly applied; for this is the immortal basely exchanged for the mortal."[5] In other words, "To choose the lower life is gratuitous pain; to choose the higher life is pruning which leads to eternal life."[6]

Pruning means cutting away the dead and unnecessary, that is, whatever feeds the old nature. It means there are things we will be called upon to give up for the sake of the kingdom. And as we lose our life, our own will, our own way, and our own pleasure for Christ's sake, we discover the real life that only Christ can give. It comes down to priorities.

To begin to distinguish the priorities associated with lower and higher living, we end this section with comparisons between the two natures.

LIVING FOR NOW VS. WAITING UPON THE LORD

A priority of the old nature is to be present-oriented. We are told to eat, drink, and be merry, for tomorrow we die. By not seeing beyond the immediate, the world fails to see the benefit of waiting for the ripened fruit. A wise Christian friend once told me, "I try not to speak, buy or react on impulse. To do so generally gratifies an immediate desire, but it may be a desire of the flesh or Satan."

The Holy Spirit uses the natural course of time and events to confirm His will in our lives. That is why we are told time and time again in Scripture to wait upon the Lord. Our new nature is future-oriented, keeping eternal values in focus. It is willing to be subjected to the discipline of God.

5. Joseph S. Exell, *The Biblical Illustrator* (Grand Rapids: Baker, 1973), p. 194.
6. George Arthur Buttrick, *The Interpreter's Bible*, vol. 7 (Nashville: Abingdon, 1951), p. 376.

SELF-SUFFICIENCY VS. DEPENDENCE UPON GOD

The old nature promotes self-sufficiency—we must pull ourselves up by our own "bootstraps." We must be number one; we must be kings. As we can discover from reading the story of the rich young ruler in Matthew 19, by-products of self-sufficiency are pride and anger. (See chapter 7 for an in-depth look at that passage.) Although many of us may not feel self-sufficient financially, we still reflect a self-sufficient attitude. Our actions and relationships declare that we do not need God.

The spiritual man, whose new nature is controlled by the Holy Spirit, rejoices in his dependence on God. We Christians must throw ourselves recklessly upon God and prepare to surrender unto death all our ambitions, plans, and possessions. We must never claim glory for anything we are or have. We must never make conditions for our willingness to serve. Our allegiance is total, and our desire for His glory is supreme.

SELF-IMAGE

Of all the areas of psychology, the topic of self-image and self-worth has been distorted more than any other. The reason for that and many other distortions relates to the humanistic perspective, which defies man. Jay Adams points out,

> Notions of the importance of a good self-concept, identity, and self-esteem are widespread today. Theorists, who misunderstand the biblical way of Christ, are perpetually insisting that one cannot love others until first he has come to love himself. His self image must be adequate before he can reach out to others.[7]

Even well-known Christian speakers and teachers have gotten caught up in this subtle humanistic trap. Again, Jay Adams says,

> A realistic self-evaluation is good but impossible for those who do not have the Bible for their yardstick. Self-acceptance is possible only in Christ, in whom God accepts forgiven sinners. Yet a realistic self-evaluation can lead only to non-acceptance of oneself and the determination that he must repent and be changed.[8]

7. Jay Adams, *The Christian Counselor's Manual* (Philadelphia: Pres. & Ref., 1975), p. 145.
8. Ibid.

Apart from the transforming work of the Holy Spirit there can be no lasting self acceptance, because it is all too easy for a nonbeliever (or even a believer who is not well grounded) to fall prey to a phenomenon known as "the self-fulfilling prophesy." Simply put, that basically means, "I am what I think you think I am." In other words, who I am and how much I'm worth is contingent upon the opinions of others. If I come to the conclusion that another person thinks of me as good and important, then my self-image is enlarged; if I perceive that another person detests me, my self image is deflated. Whether or not my perceptions are correct does not matter. As I think how I am considered to be, that I become. Dr. Paul Brand comments along the same lines: "In our Western societies, the worth of persons is determined by how much society is willing to pay for their services. Living in such a society, my vision gets clouded. I begin viewing janitors as having less human worth than jet pilots."[9]

THE SELF-FULFILLING PROPHECY

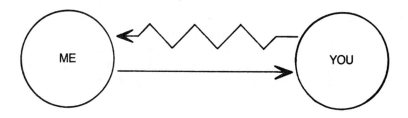

In contrast, Scripture teaches that our self-image need not go up and down like a yo-yo, for it can have the stability that is found in Christ alone. As a believer, I look to God who loves me far more and far better than I can ever love myself.

9. Paul Brand and Philip Yancey, *Fearfully and Wonderfully Made* (Grand Rapids: Zondervan, 1980), pp. 38-39.

See how great a love the Father has bestowed upon us, that we should be called children of God; and such we are. For this reason the world does not know us, because it did not know Him. Beloved, now we are children of God, and it has not appeared as yet what we shall be. We know that, when He appears, we shall be like Him, because we shall see Him just as He is. And everyone who has this hope fixed on Him purifies himself, just as He is pure. (1 John 3:1-3)

In this is love, not that we loved God, but that He loved us and sent His Son to be the propitiation for our sins. . . . And we have come to know and have believed the love which God has for us. God is love, and the one who abides in love abides in God, and God abides in him. By this, love is perfected with us, that we may have confidence in the day of judgment; because as He is, so also are we in this world. There is no fear in love; but perfect love casts out fear, because fear involves punishment, and the one who fears is not perfected in love. We love, because He first loved us. (4:10, 16-19)

These verses stress *knowing* God's love through Christ, *abiding* in that love, being *perfected* in that love, having *confidence* in that love, and *losing our fear* in that love. The bottom line here is that the stability of our self-image is no longer dependent on mental gymnastics; it is grounded in the Father's *deep, perfect, unchanging* love for us because of our relationship to Him through Jesus Christ. What release and freedom that gives us in all our relationships! No matter how others respond to us, we are able to respond to them freely and safely, surrounded by His love and reaching out through His love.

THE BIBLICAL VIEW OF SELF

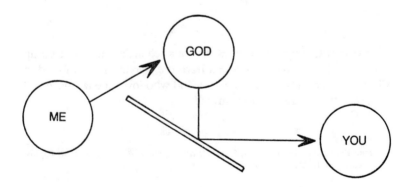

Our identity becomes totally wrapped up in Him—in His forgiveness, His faithfulness, His commands, and His glory. We lose ourselves in Him and, in doing so, discover that we are more worthy and more important and more esteemed than we ever dreamed possible. Consequently, we are able to reflect our secure and stable identity on to others.

The Bible has much to say about how we are to regard ourselves. The following are only some examples.

- Isaiah 41:6-10: Self-image and security come from God and others.
- Matthew 16:24: We are to deny (lit., "disown") self.
- John 15:5: Apart from God, we can do nothing.
- Romans 6:11: We should consider ourselves dead to sin.
- Romans 7:18: Nothing good dwells in us.
- Romans 11:18: We do not support the root; the root supports us.
- Romans 12:10, 16: Give preference to another, be of the same mind, do not think we are too good for someone.
- Romans 14:7-8: We do not live or die for ourselves—we are the Lord's.
- Romans 15:3: Even Christ did not please Himself.
- 1 Corinthians 3:7: He who plants, waters, and so on is nothing—only God is.
- 1 Corinthians 12:7: Each of us is given manifestation of the Spirit for the common good.
- 1 Corinthians 13:2: If we have no love for others, we are not worth anything.
- 2 Corinthians 3:4ff.: We are not adequate in ourselves; adequacy comes from God.
- 2 Corinthians 5:17: All things (including our self-image) become new in Christ.
- Philippians 2:3-4: We must do nothing from selfish motives, but rather show humility, realizing that others are more important than ourselves.

STUDY QUESTIONS

1. It was pointed out that the majority of people are likely to fall prey to the self-fulfilling prophesy. Give some examples of how we Christians often judge our self-worth in that way.

2. Jay Adams states that a non-Christian cannot have a realistic self appraisal. Do you agree with his assessment? Why or why not?

3. How is it possible not to be influenced by the priorities set for us by our culture? Give a specific plan for accomplishing that.

4. Can you think of more comparisons that can be made between the new nature and the old nature?

5. Taking the list of verses that deal with our self-image (presented at the end of the chapter), summarize them into one paragraph entitled "The Biblical View of Self."

12

To Die Is to Live

But when this perishable will have put on the imperishable, and this mortal will have put on immortality, then will come about the saying that is written, "Death is swallowed up in victory. O death, where is your victory? O death, where is your sting?" The sting of death is sin, and the power of sin is the law; But thanks be to God who gives us the victory through our Lord Jesus Christ.

—1 Corinthians 15:54-57

Richard DeHaan of the Radio Bible Class recalls a childhood incident that his father made use of to teach him the meaning of the above passage. One day he and his brother were walking in a field with their father when a bee flew up and stung him just above the eye. Richard quickly brushed it away and threw himself in the grass, screaming for help. The bee then went straight for Richard's brother, Marvin, and began to buzz around his head. Panic-stricken, Marvin also started yelling to his father for help.

Coming to the boys' rescue, Dr. DeHaan picked up Marvin and told him to stop crying. "That bee is harmless," his father assured him. It can't hurt you. It has lost its sting. The bee can still scare you, but it is powerless to hurt you. Your brother took the sting away by being stung." He then used the event to graphically explain this passage in Corinthians. "Christ," he said, "had taken the sting of death, our sin, and had borne its penalty for us on Calvary's cross. When we are willing for the Holy Spirit to teach us, He often uses everyday happenings."[1]

In my own life, the impact of this paradox, "to die is to live," really sank in when as a college student I had the opportunity to work at a funeral home. From that experience I was made vividly aware that the physical body is a mere outer shell for that true essence of the individual that lives eternally.

As a licensed apprentice embalmer, I prepared bodies for the funeral service and subsequent burial. As I worked with the bodies, I was struck time and time again with the realization that that was exactly *all* I was working with—a discarded shell.

During my summer days at the mortuary, I witnessed many funerals. Some were Christian; some were not. I concluded one thing from observing those services: Christians seem to slip easily into the world's thinking on the subject of death. Everything from ordering the higher-priced casket with a more secure seal for the purpose of preservation, to viewing the deceased as if the shell were the real person, to worrying that the departed one would not be happy with the grave site surroundings were the marks of Christian as well as non-Christian funerals.

In almost every other area of the Christian walk we accept the fact that we are different from the world. But the more I became involved in the mortuary business, the more I wondered why so many believers hang on to the non-Christian perspective of death as an event to be dreaded and feared.

The paradox thus develops. The Bible teaches that death is the key, the doorway to eternal, perfect life. And for the Christian, even though it is still an enemy, physical death will ultimately bring glory, eternal happiness, and communion with God. To the nonbeliever, however, that joyful promise appears to be only a vague placater of fear, and death seems overwhelmingly final.

DEATH IS OUR ENEMY

Dr. Thomas T. Frantz of the Life and Death Transition Center at the State University of New York at Buffalo states, "The subconscious fear of death is the one constant in everyone's life, regardless of station. Whether we realize it or not, death influences just about every deci-

---

1. Dennis J. DeHaan, *Windows on the Word* (Grand Rapids: Radio Bible Class, 1984), pp. 37-38.

sion we make and every action we take."[2]

Yet due to the highly emotional nature of the subject, death is a difficult issue to address. The Bible, however, speaks much of death. In fact, there are over eight hundred references related to death and dying in Scripture.

Death is the ultimate curse on man for sin. It is the penalty that both the Christian and the non-Christian must pay. Scripture, as we have seen, openly declares death to be an enemy. According to the bylaws of the Garden, the penalty for eating from the Tree of the Knowledge of Good and Evil was death. The process begun on that infamous day and recorded in Genesis 3 has equalized every human being since, "as it is appointed for men to die once" (Hebrews 9:27).

The sorrow that comes with death is a part of our human experience. No matter how much we wish otherwise and no matter how hard we fight against it, our friends and family and we ourselves face this inevitable foe. And because the average person fears sorrow, especially the sorrow of death, the tendency is to refuse to look it in the face until it strikes close to home.

Even though Christ did not fear death, He could not remain untouched by the sorrow of this nemesis. At the death of His friend Lazarus, Scripture says that "Jesus wept" (John 11:35). Even though Christ knew that Lazarus would be raised again momentarily, the tragedy of death overcame Him. Later, in the Garden of Gethsemane, we find Him recoiling at the pain and suffering of His own death. On the cross, death and the separation from His Father caused not only physical but emotional pain as well.

No, death is not a friend. It is an enemy that causes people of all ages, through every means available, to resist its coming. Sooner or later it must come, but we believers live in the joyful knowledge that Christ has bought the ultimate victory over death through His resurrection. Knowing that, the apostle Paul could exclaim, "Death, where is your victory . . . and where is your sting?"

THE CHRISTIAN VIEW OF DEATH

To properly appreciate the Christian posture toward death, we must first remind ourselves of how the rest of the world views it. Death, defined according to the prevailing humanistic thinking of our age, is (1) an absence of self-awareness, (2) an inability to relate to

2. Thomas T. Frantz, "Death in America: No Longer a Hidden Subject," *US News and World Report,* 13 November 1978, p. 68.

others, and (3) a lack of rational thinking.[3] That definition unfortunately permits abortion and euthanasia without guilt.

Many in our society would stop short of calling themselves humanists, yet they adapt to its mind-sets almost unknowingly. And according to the tenets of humanism, there is no life after death. Consequently, we are encouraged to live it up while we can and grab all the gusto, because while there may be a heaven, there certainly is not a hell.

When the believer declares that our lives today do make a difference in our eternal destination—that dying to self now is the path to real life, eternal life—the nonbeliever views such talk as a quizzical paradox or perhaps, as Sigmund Freud declared, a manipulative dogma.

It is easy to see the void that the humanistic perspective reflects. But how can we believers combat that mushrooming mind-set? To answer that question, we must ask and answer three interwoven questions: Why must we die? Is there more than one type of death? and What does the Bible say by way of instruction on this topic?

WHY MUST WE DIE?

Death, we must remember, is an enemy, and it is a constant reminder and result of sin. We must die because of the original sin recorded in the book of Genesis. Adam and Eve are given a warning: if they disobey God, they will die (2:17). Satan lies to them, saying that they will be just like God if they eat of the tree (3:4-5). The Fall occurs (3:6-7), and God pronounces the sentence of spiritual and physical death, plus additional penalties: to Eve, sorrow, pain, and submission to her husband; to Adam, hard work, thorns, weeds—a constant reminder of his action (3:16-19).

The sin of Adam and Eve set in motion the Adamic sentence, which is passed upon all mankind. The apostle Paul reflects on that when he writes, "Therefore, just as through one man sin entered into the world, and death through sin, and so death spread to all men, because all sinned" (Romans 5:12). And, "If Christ is in you . . . the body is dead because of sin" (8:10).

3. James C. Coleman, *Contemporary Psychology and Effective Behavior*, 4th ed. (Glenview, Ill.: Scott, Foresman, 1974), p. 40.
4. The Humanist Manifesto, which outlines the tenets of humanism, is critiqued by Nancy Barcus in "The Humanist Builds His House on the Sand," *Moody Monthly*, September 1980, pp. 24-30.

We may be believers, but our bodies are still under the Adamic sentence.

THREE KINDS OF DEATH MENTIONED IN THE BIBLE

When Adam and Eve sinned against God, the death monster emerged triple-headed. The first head is spiritual death. Jesus frequently mentioned that kind of death. For example, He said, "Truly, truly, I say to you, he who hears My word, and believes Him who sent Me, has eternal life, and does not come into judgment, but has passed out of death into life" (John 5:24). And Paul tells the Ephesians, "You were dead in your trespasses and sins" (Ephesians 2:1). Those passages help us understand that we are born spiritually dead and thus separated from God.

The second head of the monster is physical death. Physical death comes at different times and ways to every individual, but, as Paul declares, we all have the sentence of death in ourselves. Yet Scripture never teaches us to throw up our hands in the face of death, defeated and discouraged. Alexander Schmemann in his book *For the Life of the World* writes, "Christianity is not reconciliation with death. It is the revelation of death, and it reveals death because it is the revelation of Life. And only if Christ is Life, is death what Christianity proclaims it to be, namely the enemy to be destroyed, and not a 'mystery' to be explained."[5]

Christianity does not deny death, but secularism ironically counsels acceptance yet attempts to ignore death or to domesticate it (thus we have "funeral homes" to make it seem less horrible than it is). Again Schmemann: "It is when Life weeps at the grave of the friend, when it contemplates the horror of death, that the victory over death begins."[6] Secularism has no weapons against death; Christianity transforms death into life.

There is yet a third head of death mentioned in Scripture. It is what the Bible calls the "second death." The second death is another term for the lake of fire—eternal separation from God in a literal place He has designed for those who have not received Him as Savior and Lord.

The second death comes after the great white throne judgment, spoken of in Revelation.

---

5. Alexander Schmemann's quote was extracted from an article written by Rodney Clapp, entitled, "Dying as a Way of Life," *Christianity Today,* 18 March 1983, p. 12.
6. Ibid.

> Blessed and holy is the one who has a part in the first resurrection;
> over these the second death has no power, but they will be priests
> of God and of Christ and will reign with Him for a thousand years. . .
> And death and Hades were thrown into the lake of fire. This is the
> second death, the lake of fire. (Revelation 20:6, 14)

Have you ever wondered why a Christian's death is often referred to in Scripture as "falling asleep" (e.g., 1 Corinthians 15:6)? That does not mean that Christians are in a state of limbo after death. What it does indicate, however, is that God looks on the believer as having life with Him for eternity after death occurs.

Commenting on Paul's statement that "we shall not all sleep" (1 Corinthians 15:51), Harry A. Ironside writes,

> He [Paul] uses the word 'sleep' in place of 'die,' for death to the be-
> liever is the putting of the tired, weary, worn body to sleep until the
> Lord Jesus comes to waken it again. It is only the body that sleeps.
> The real man, the spirit and soul, is absent from the body and prese-
> nt with the Lord, taken home to be with Christ, which is far better,
> so that the bodies of our friends in Christ who have died are sleep-
> ing, but they themselves are with Christ, wonderfully happy in His
> Presence.[7]

BIBLICAL ADMONITIONS ON THE TOPIC OF DEATH

To help us clarify our thoughts on the biblical teaching of death, there are seven points to consider.

ALL LIFE OPERATES IN CYCLES

From the flowers in our garden to the four seasons of the year, all life, including human life, is affected by cycles. All cycles start out with a birth and conclude with death.

One might ask, Why does the universe operate in cycles? We can deduce from the book of Genesis that cycles are a result of the Adamic sentence. Cycles are always a reminder of mortal imperfection. Hypothetically, had Adam and Eve not sinned, many theologians believe their lives would have been enriched and prolonged on a continuum throughout eternity. However, once sin entered the picture, there came the surety of an end to all things. Solomon expressed this thought:

7. Harry A. Ironside, *The First Epistle to the Corinthians* (New York: Loizeaux, 1938), pp. 522-25.

There is an appointed time for everything.
And there is a time for every event under heaven—
A time to give birth, and a time to die;
A time to plant, and a time to uproot what is planted.
A time to kill, and a time to heal;
A time to tear down, and a time to build up.
A time to weep, and a time to laugh;
A time to mourn, and a time to dance.

(Ecclesiastes 3:1-4)

Only God Himself and eternity are not affected by cycles, for Scripture tells us that God always was (eternity past) and will always be (eternity future). And even though God is not bound by cycles He controls them. As He states in the book of Isaiah: "I am God, and there is no one like Me, declaring the end from the beginning and from ancient times things which have not been done, saying, My purpose will be established, and I will accomplish all My good pleasure" (Isaiah 46:9b-10).

Death does complete the cycle of physical life. But with that completion comes the non-changing state of eternity for all men, wherein cycles will cease to exist. For the believer, life with God will be enriched and prolonged on a continuum throughout the ages. For the nonbeliever, life apart from God will be characterized by an ever present torment and suffering in hell.

WE ARE JUST SOJOURNERS, PASSING THROUGH THIS WORLD

The apostle Peter writes, "And if ye call on the Father, who without respect of persons judgeth according to every man's work, pass the time of your sojourning here in fear" (1 Peter 1:17). The word translated "sojourning" implies a state of non-permanence, a picture that the writer to the Hebrews paints when he says:

By faith Abraham, when he was called to go out into a place which he should after receive an inheritance, obeyed; and he went out, not knowing whither he went. By faith he sojourned in the land of promise, as in a strange country, dwelling in tabernacles with Isaac and Jacob, the heirs with him on the same promise: for he looked [or waited] for a city which hath foundations, whose builder and maker is God. (Hebrews 11:8-10, KJV)

Sojourning thus carries the idea of traveling through a foreign country. As was the case with Abraham, we ought not settle into this earth in such a way as to cease yearning for our true home.

APART FROM BEING ABLE TO SERVE THE LORD, BEING ABSENT FROM THIS BODY IS
MUCH BETTER

The apostle Paul writes to the Philippians:

> For to me, to live is Christ, and to die is gain. But if I am to live on in
> the flesh, this will mean fruitful labor for me; and I do not know
> which to choose. But I am hard-pressed from both directions, hav-
> ing the desire to depart and be with Christ, for that is very much
> better; yet to remain on in the flesh is more necessary for your sake.
> (Philippians 1:21-24)

Several years ago I conducted a funeral for an eighteen-year-old
Christian girl. While I was preparing for the message, I began to pon-
der the impact of the above passage and was forced to ask myself, *Do
I really believe what Paul is saying here? Is it really possible to so
long for heaven that there is a debate that goes on in my mind over
the issue?*

Paul was not suicidal, nor did he desire to escape from society. He
is not stating in this passage that the act of dying was far better than
living. Rather, "to have died" is the more appropriate meaning; the
change of state caused by death is much better than mortal life.

I can get so involved with the things of life, even good things, that I
can loose the real reason for my existence, which is to some day be
with my Heavenly Father. To have Paul's perspective on heaven is
thus a guarantee for joy, happiness, and hope while going through difficult times. To be wrapped up in the things of this world will result
in depression, a lack of security, and tension.

GOD HAS THE ULTIMATE POWER OVER DEATH, BECAUSE HE CONQUERED IT BY
DYING AND RISING FROM THE DEAD

The prophet Isaiah reflected this truth when he wrote, "He will
swallow up death for all time, and the Lord God will wipe tears away
from all faces, and He will remove the reproach of His people from all
the earth; for the Lord has spoken" (Isaiah 25:8). The prophet Hosea
also echoed the thought: "I will ransom them from the power of Sheol [the grave]; I will redeem them from death. O Death, where are
your thorns? O Sheol, where is your sting? Compassion will be hidden
from My sight" (Hosea 13:14). And in Hebrews 2:14-15 we read,

"Since then the children share in flesh and blood, He Himself likewise also partook of the same, that through death He might render powerless him who had the power of death, that is, the devil; and might deliver those who through fear of death were subject to slavery all their lives.

Those verses conclude that for a period of time God permitted Satan to have the power to enslave a vast majority of mankind through the fear of death. Then, in the fullness of time, God the Father sent Jesus Christ the Son, who willingly took on the form of man. Not only did He share in flesh and blood, but He partook also of that which had for so long enslaved mankind—He partook of death. And through His resurrection triumph our Lord Jesus, in one victorious sweep, took the captor captive and rendered his ultimate weapon— death— impotent.

DEATH IS THE KEY TO PERFECTION

In Revelation 21:4 we are told, "And He shall wipe away every tear from their eyes; and there shall no longer be any death; there shall no longer be any mourning, or crying, or pain; the first things [or the former things] have passed away." What is John referring to when he talks about the "former things?" They are the consequences of Genesis 3—the Adamic curse. In eternity that penalty will be lifted forever. If we did not die, we would remain imperfect, continually susceptible to all the troubles of life. But because of death we can be made perfect. The affects of sin, which have polluted the genes of mankind since Adam, will no longer have power over us.

WE ARE EXPECTED TO SORROW OVER THE LOSS OF A LOVED ONE, BUT NOT DISPROPORTIONATELY

"But we do not want you to be uninformed, brethren, about those who are asleep, that you may not grieve, as do the rest who have no hope" (1 Thessalonians 4:13). Grief is not to be abolished, nor can it be, because we are emotional creatures. However, our grief should not reach the magnitude of many non-Christians throughout the world, who, without hope, mourn for long periods of time and even inflict bodily harm upon themselves during times of bereavement.

Several years ago my family had the privilege of touring Irian Jaya, where my brother and his family were serving as missionaries. My brother took us into the interior to see the people they had been working with for fifteen years. During our stay we trekked over the countryside, observing the culture of the Ok Bap people. As we hiked along the mountain pathways, my brother would contrast the present times with when he first arrived. He said that before many of the tribe became Christians they were involved in spirit worship, and the control of Satan on their lives was evident. At death, my brother stated, the surviving spouse would cut off a finger in a ritual of mourning. The wailing and anguish could be heard for miles, he said, as the family members, almost in an emotional frenzy, yelped out for hours and in some cases days over the loss of a loved one. Since the early days of my brother's ministry in Irian Jaya, however, he has seen many of those same tribespeople, because of Christianity, change their death rituals.

A second passage here may also help us to understand the role of grief in the loss of a loved one. The story relates how David handled grief when he found out that his baby had died.

> So David arose from the ground, washed, anointed himself, and changed his clothes; and he came into the house of the Lord and worshiped. Then he came to his own house, and when he requested, they set food before him and he ate. Then his servants said to him, "What is this thing that you have done? While the child was alive, you fasted and wept; but when the child died, you arose and ate food." And he said, "While the child was alive, I fasted and wept; for I said, 'Who knows, the Lord may be gracious to me, that the child may live.' But now he has died; why should I fast? Can I bring him back again? I shall go to him, but he will not return to me." (2 Samuel 12:20-23)

I have counseled Christians who felt guilty because they did not experience immediate "victory" at the death of a spouse. When I see that occurring, I usually give the following analogy. If I break an arm, the doctor needs to set it and place it in a cast; it will take approximately six weeks for it to heal. Once the cast is removed, the rehabilitation process must continue, due to the disuse of the arm over that period of time. And no matter how hard I would like to speed up the healing process, it takes time to get well. So it is at the death of a loved one. It is like having an appendage break. We cannot with a snap of our fingers dismiss our grief and go on with life as if the death did not occur. However, with a Scriptural foundation of a clear picture of eternity, the rehabilitation process can proceed without the obstructions of a mind-set that is void of hope.

GOD USES DEATH AS A FORM OF REMEMBRANCE

God wants us to keep in our minds the importance of what He has done for us by sending Christ into the world to die and rise again in order that we too can have victory over death. Is that not what Communion is all about? "For as often as you eat this bread and drink the cup, you proclaim the Lord's death until He comes" (1 Corinthians 11:26). As the Jews of old were to wear a headband (Deuteronomy 6) to remind them of God's laws, so by communion we remind ourselves of Christ's work at Calvary. And because of His victory, it is now possible for us to have victory over death as well.

Christ's death and resurrection, then, provide the believer with hope and comfort. And with that in mind, how we live today is affected in a very real way. "But thanks be to God, who gives us the victory through our Lord Jesus Christ. Therefore, my beloved brethren, be steadfast, immovable, always abounding in the work of the Lord, knowing that your toil is not in vain in the Lord" (1 Corinthians 15:57-58).

Dying in Order to Live

Scripture indicates much about heaven, the new Jerusalem where the streets will be paved with gold and where eternal life will bring all of our highest hopes to fulfillment. The Christian perspective on death is not a "pie in the sky by and by" religion; Christianity is built on a complete trust in the historic Jesus Christ who died and arose from the grave almost twenty centuries ago. The day I understood and accepted that death as being for me, I died spiritually to an old life; and I, like Jesus, was resurrected to a new life. So I now say that I live "in Christ," as the New Testament repeatedly reminds us. The moment I experienced that, my mind ascended to a new level of awareness, including peace with my limited daily existence and certainty of a future life.

Christianity uses the term "new birth" to describe how entirely new we become when we accept Christ as our Savior and Lord. Our old nature is put to death, and we have glorious new life in Christ (Romans 6:4). For those of us who are believers, a very significant part of us has already died, and we have experienced spiritual resurrection. In Colossians 3:3 Paul says, "For you have died and your [real] life is hidden with Christ in God." So when our physical death comes, it is not a total change. It is simply the completion of a process that began when we accepted Christ as Savior.

When I was a child in Central America, there once came the news of five young men who were martyred for Christ in Ecuador. In the course of the memorial service, the victory theme came through loud and clear. One of the slain missionaries' wives had written a poem entitled "The Other Side":

> This is not death—it's glory;
> It isn't dark—it's light;
> It isn't stumbling, groping, or even faith—it's sight;
> This isn't grief—it's having my last tear wiped away;
> It is sunrise—the morning of my eternal day;
> This isn't praying—its speaking face to face, and it's
>   glimpsing at all the wonders of his grace;
> This is the end of all pleading for strength to bear
>   my pain; not even pain's dark memory will ever
>   live again;
> How did I bear the earth life before I came up high-
>   er? before my soul was granted its every deep
>   desire? before I knew this rapture of meeting
>   face to face with that one who sought me, saved
>   me, and kept me by His grace?
> This is not death—it's glory![8]

Many Christians cannot share that degree of hope, because although God has rescued them from the domain of darkness (Colossians 1:13), considerable darkness remains. Even though death was defeated on the cross, death continues to cast its shadow. How important it is for us to realize that death is exactly that—a shadow. My children like to turn on the slide projector and play finger shadow games on the screen. The fingers held just so cast a shadow resembling a snake, a bird, or a lion. But there is no real lion or bird. Just as our fingers belong to us, death now belongs to us in Christ. And who should be afraid of his own shadow?

Yet, of course, we are. The darkness remains greatly, if not ultimately, fearsome. Even here, however, we have a solace and hope. Christ Jesus follows us into the dark night of the soul, and when darkness engulfs us it only means He has encompassed the darkness.

---

8. The poem was extracted from the memorial service held at the Bible Institute of Shell Mera and broadcast live over HCJB, Quito, Ecuador, one week after the death of the five missionaries (21 January 1956).

STUDY QUESTIONS

1. In planning a funeral for a departed believer, what would you include? What would you not include? Why?
2. Do you agree with Dr. Frantz's assessment that death influences almost every decision we make and every action we take? Why or why not?
3. How does humanistic philosophy define death? How is it different from the Christian perspective?
4. What are the three kinds of death brought into being when Adam and Eve sinned?
5. Psychologists tell us that all survivors go through the following four steps when a loved one dies: *denial/shock* (numbness, search for loved one, guilt feelings, anger, and depression); *adjustment-mourning* (saying good-by, new life without partner, making decisions by ones self, a let-up of grief); *transition* (accept what could not be accepted in step 1, learning to operate with amputation); and *growth* (new identity, slow return to normal state). Do you think that those stages (involving guilt feelings, anger, depression, and so on) are all necessary for a mature Christian?